CHAMPIONSHIP PRAISE FOR THE RENTAL GAME

"If you want something done right, turn to a professional. The Rental Game quickly points out the pitfalls of going alone. Renting your home is an important decision with significant financial implications that should not be taken casually. Before you decide to rent your home, you owe it to yourself to read the Rental Game. This book is filled with tips, insightful advice, "war stories" and more. If you plan to rent, you'll be glad you read this book first."

Rick Dacri, President
Dacri & Associates, LLC

"I have been traveling mid-week non-stop since getting your book in the mail. I finally had a chance to read it on the way back from Santa Fe today. WOW!!! You have done a major Mitzvah for our industry! I am sure your friends at VRMA mobbed you to thank them. Any owner of a vacation home needs to read this book!

LOVED IT!!! I am going to tell every client I see that they should buy a copy for all new owners and prospects!"

Doug Kennedy, President
Kennedy Training Network, LLC

"This book contains a powerhouse of information on an important aspect of my real estate business, the second home market as investment properties. Having sold many vacation rental properties over the last 14 years, I look forward to sharing your well written book with my past clients and what a great way to reconnect by sharing a copy of your book! It really identifies the trials and tribulations that go with owning and managing vacation rentals."

Gregory Gosselin, Broker/Owner
Gosselin Realty Group

THE RENTAL GAME

Winning with a Professional Vacation Rental Team

Maureen Regan

DISCLAIMER

The information contained in this book is meant to assist a vacation homeowner or real estate professional to choose the right professional vacation rental agency and to understand why the vacation rental commission they pay is worth the cost. It also points out the difficulties of renting and managing your own vacation rental property. This book should allow each person to learn what they need to know to make an informed decision.

This book is not meant as a primer for Vacation Rental Managers or individuals; however, there is much to learn in the book that can assist the dedicated professional. There are certainly a lot of great ideas out there and the ones mentioned in this book are but a few. My goal is to give you an overview of what I think works.

DEDICATION

There are lots of great professionals, owners and guests associated with this business. Many have shared their stories and ideas within these pages. I am immensely thankful to all of them. Those businesses mentioned in the book, as well as others, are listed in the resource guide should you wish to contact them. Also our website, **www.the-rental-game.com**, carries on the conversations started in this book.

My love and gratitude to Dan, Jennifer, Jude, Annette, Margaret, Patrick, Aidan, Jack, Alex and always, Armosa. Thanks to the amazing staff at Seaside Vacation Rentals, Robert, Donna, Patti, Kevin, Steve, Trisha, Sandi and Chulani.

THE RENTAL GAME

CHAPTER 1

INTRODUCTION

Sometimes A Little Knowledge Is a Dangerous Thing

We all want to think we can do everything and often we don't even realize we've made a mistake until after it's happened. I grew up in a French-Canadian family, so I know how to speak <u>some</u> French. When I bought my first new car, the salesman asked me if I knew French and of course, I said yes. He told me to ask the mechanics, who spoke only French, to change my license plate from my old wreck to the new car. I won't repeat what I said in French, but when I left there, all the mechanics were laughing hysterically. Afterwards, I asked my grandmother what they were laughing about. She, too, began to laugh and cry at the same time. When she finally stopped, she told me I had asked them to change out my prostitute's license! Sometimes it's just better to know your limitations.

Maureen Regan
Seaside Vacation Rentals, York, Maine

INTRODUCTION

GET YOUR GAME ON

THIS BOOK IS FOR YOU if you own a property and are considering renting for short term rentals. My intention with the book is to help you to weigh the pros and cons of managing this rental property yourself or whether hiring a vacation rental manager would be your best choice.

It's also for you if you are a realtor or vacation rental manager who wants to be able to determine best practices for vacation rentals.

I believe, after reading this book, you will choose a professional vacation rental manager. Yes, I am biased! I have rented my own property and have owned a vacation rental business since 1983 and so I speak from a wealth of experience. I have also drawn from the experiences of owners, guests and leaders in the vacation rental management industry. I hope you will agree with me by the end of this book that a vacation rental professional is the best way to win **The Rental Game**. And the best vacation rental professionals want **YOU** as part of the 'Team' that manages your property.

As Betsy LaBarge, of Mt Hood Rentals in Welches, OR says,
-    *"The reality? Vacation rental managers work with property owners as partners. Of course, vacation rental managers need to have systems and routines to run an organized and cost-effective business, but they also need to remember that the property owner is their*

partner in business and that there would not be a business without the property owner. And for a property owner, many of the headaches of owning a second home go away with management."

So, I leave it up to you. Tally up the scorecard at the end of this book and **YOU** decide how to play **The Rental Game** to **WIN!**

FIRST THINGS FIRST... WHAT ARE VACATION RENTALS?

They are individually owned homes and condos. Vacation rental properties are located all over the world in every desirable tourist area. They can rent for a night, a week, a month or longer. They are a wonderful way to vacation and most folks who have tried it will come back year after year. Rentals offer so many advantages including the fact that they are economical, a great way for families and friends to get together under one roof. They have many amenities, including a kitchen that a hotel room or other type of accommodation may not offer; they provide privacy, unique decor and great locations.

THE REASON FOR 'THE RENTAL GAME'
This book came about after looking through several bookstores to present a prospective new rental owner with a book on professionally managed vacation home renting. I've been in the vacation rental business for 30 years and I came away frustrated, finding that no such book existed. However, there were books extolling homeowners to "do it themselves" without all the facts. While vacation renting certainly can be done by an individual homeowner, and I have seen it done quite well occasionally, it is more often not done well or becomes an overwhelming burden for the owners.

Doing it yourself is certainly not a decision to be taken lightly.

As Royal Shell Vacation Rentals' Vice President, Ben Edwards said,

- *"Choosing a Vacation Manager to professionally market, maintain and manage your vacation rental is an investment. In most every case, professional Vacation Rental Managers will out-perform non-Vacation Rental Managers while maintaining a significantly higher level of service and standards for the subject property."*

SO YOU WANT TO PLAY THE RENTAL GAME? THESE ARE THE RULES…

If you own or are thinking of buying a vacation home that you want to rent for part or all of the year, you will find within these pages many reasons why using a professional agency may be your best bet and make you more money than doing it yourself. And if you are a real estate agent, you will find a way to seek out a valuable partnership with a vacation rental professional.

The very best time to consider a professional rental agency is _before_ you buy that vacation home. Even if renting is something you may do in the distant future you will want to have all the facts ahead of time before acting on that purchase. I recommend seeing a professional rental agency because they can help you to determine before you buy, the areas that will rent best, the size and makeup of house that the market demands and many other factors. Also, they may have a real estate arm of their business that can work with you if you are not already working with a realtor. That affiliate probably specializes in the sale of vacation rental properties. They can also recommend a real estate professional in the area.

If you are working with a real estate agent to find a property, ask questions about their affiliations with vacation rental management companies. The best way to achieve your goal of a buying a highly rentable property is to be working with a team made up of a really good real estate agent and a really good vacation rental professional.

By the way, laws vary from state to state on how vacation rental agencies must be licensed and whether or not they are controlled by the state's real estate commission. Currently, about fifteen to twenty states do not require that rental agencies be licensed by the real estate commission, which you should not equate as being a bad thing.

For companies that do real estate only, I suggest seeking out the best vacation rental agency in your area and working out an agreement that will benefit your client and both of your companies.

Seaside frequently receives calls from agents in our area with buyers looking to purchase a vacation rental home. We are happy to help out any real estate agent by being able to evaluate a property, give rental comparables and renting information to their client. To protect the agent for the future, should that buyer become one of our renting homeowners and later decide to sell, we note in our files what agent sent that homeowner to us and always refer them back to the agent. The larger benefit to the agent is that bringing us in to meet with the potential buyer, always helps with closing the deal. It's great for a buyer to have two experts working for them instead of only one!

So, when you start searching for a property to be used as a vacation rental, do your homework and find the right vacation rental agency linked with the right real estate company to help you out first.

CHAPTER 2

MYTHS AND REALITIES: MIND GAMES

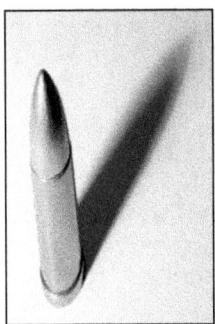

File this one under funny-strange!

One day, while some guests were at the beach, their son found a .50 caliber shell on the beach that has washed up from a military machine gun. A 50 caliber shell is about 6 inches long and considered one of the most deadly weapons used by our military.

Ben Edwards, Vice President
Royal Shell Vacations, Florida

MYTHS AND REALITIES: MIND GAMES

There are a great many myths connected with vacation renting. These exist with homeowners, guests and the general public. Let's explore these myths and reveal what is truth and what is fiction.

HOMEOWNER MYTHS:

THE COMMISSION MONSTER

Robert Kiyosaki, the author of 'Rich Dad Poor Dad', says,

- *"Great property managers create value. (They) are valuable members of your team because they specialize in your market, and they know how to maximize your investment's income-producing potential."*

However, if you ask most people, they'll tell you, "Using an agency will cost you too much money!" When homeowners and managers were surveyed as to the biggest myth, they universally gave this answer. This is probably the greatest misunderstanding in the vacation rental industry. This book will address the reality and help you see that having a vacation rental professional can actually save you a great deal of money. Consider all the elements in the chapters and weigh them yourself on the **Scorecard** in the back of the book to make your informed decision.

Alan Hammond of Holiday Vacation Rentals in Harbor Springs, Michigan offers

- *"The greatest misunderstanding owners have about using a professional manager is that it will cost them money.*

Owners often do not understand the value of using a professional management company. They might feel that using a Rental Manager is too costly without understanding the complexity of the business and the scope of "behind the scenes" work that a professional manager performs to successfully rent your home. The reality is good management companies often do not cost but pay dividends above what an owner might achieve on their own, especially if the owner places a value on their time."

- Alan also states, *"A word of advice when comparing rental management companies. Don't look for the company with the lowest fee. The fee for professional management services should be the last question in the interview process – not the first. A professional rental manager is more likely to obtain higher occupancy and rates."*

THE RENTAL GAME IS SO EASY, A 5TH GRADER COULD DO IT

I recently received an email from a vacation rental website looking to sign up individual homeowners. At least I think that's what they were trying to do. The email heading read, '5 Simple Ways to start your own Vacation Rental Business'. Really? If only I'd known these 30 years ago, it would have saved me so much work!

Bet you want to know what those 5 steps were, right? To paraphrase, they are:

1. Manage Your Properties
2. Consider Legal Requirements
3. Determine Policies
4. Understand how the Clients Reach you
5. Advertise Everywhere

To be fair, they do warn that it is not an easy thing to start a business, but you can "follow a perfect plan to succeed in this business" according to them.

Ok, so I looked at the list and realized that at the very least the 5 Simple Steps comprised the equivalent of an MBA and possibly a law degree, too.

The reality of this business is that it is NOT easy. It is exciting, challenging and really hard work – but not easy! Most of us who do it, love it, that's why we're here.

As Leigh Clarke from Railey Mountain Lake Vacations in McHenry, Maryland, says,

-   *"You have to really want to run your own business and I would caution people that I wouldn't be in this business if it weren't one of more the complex industries out there. And it is not easy. It's not easy for us. I can't imagine doing it without tools. And the kinds of decisions you make at home about caring for your home are not optional under the time pressures of having a guest there. So, I would say too that it's not what people think it's going to be, it's not managing your home. It's managing the guest experience. You have to use different resources."*

GUEST MYTHS:

VACATION RENTALS? NEVER HEARD OF THEM.

The vacation rental business is not really understood by the general public. In the US, vacation rentals are frequently not considered as a lodging option because there simply isn't a lot of information out there about this overlooked segment of the tourism trade.

In other areas of the world, vacation rental properties are the first choice with hotels a second option and it's been that way for many years.

Steve Trover, President of the Vacation Rental Managers Association and President of All Star Vacation Homes in Kissimmee, Florida, states,

- *"My hope and desire for our industry is that we become a top of line lodging option so that when someone is planning a trip they inherently, right out of the gates, don't even consider staying at a hotel first. A hotel is a secondary option, especially when it pertains to a group. So if you have more than two people you just instantly think, 'I am going to have a much better vacation if I go and stay at a vacation rental'. With that said, it is critical that our industry becomes more professional and that we operate and understand that we are hospitality professionals not just a real estate company that happens to do rentals.*

- *So where do I see it going? I see us continuing down that path and I believe we can see it already happening. In ten years we will have very professional management marketing companies that operate these properties. I think the consumer will start to think immediately, 'I'm going to go and stay with a professional management company and I'm going to stay at a vacation rental'."*

Several years ago, my sister, Margaret Regan, and I were asked to go to the United Kingdom and Ireland for six weeks to promote Maine and particularly the southern Maine Coast where my business Seaside Vacation Rentals is located.

We stayed on beyond our commitment and explored the vacation rental industry. (We've returned many times, too.) What an eye opener that initial trip was! First, they call it 'Self Catered Holidays' not vacation rentals. The 'letting' of the properties was handled very differently with what Margaret and I felt were pros in some areas and cons in others. We were able to visit with numerous companies and see many, many properties. It was a fantastic experience! We did travel shows, we met with large airlines, small hotels and many travel agencies and other sources. We worked our butts off! But I don't want to get too sidetracked from our discussion of vacation rentals here in the US.

Recently there has been a great deal of press and even a TV show featuring vacation renting in properties across the US. As a result, the public is more interested and vacation renting has grown tremendously over the last couple of years.

Guests/vacationers must be made aware that the experience they will have in a vacation rental will be very different from the uniformity of a hotel, since each place is individually owned and reflects the personality of the owner. And frankly, this is a huge part of the appeal.

- *"The reality? In our area each property is unique and decorated and outfitted at the owners personal choosing.*

- *We try very hard to make sure that each property meets the level of excellence that guests would expect at a hotel from cleanliness, to comfort, to amenities like internet and the little touches like complimentary soaps, etc".*

Amanda Hunt, President
Northwoods Camp Rentals, Greenville, Maine

MYTHS ON BOTH SIDES:

PARTY AT THE RENTED BEACH HOUSE!!! THE PLACE GETS TRASHED!

Both homeowners and guests suffer from this myth. Guests sometimes believe that it's ok to have a party, event, even a wedding before they consult with the agency.

The reality is that this occurs very infrequently. In our company, like many others, we remind guests at numerous points along the way to booking that only 6 or 8 or the maximum number of people is allowed. We remind them that anything over that number must be cleared with us and we must obtain written permission from the homeowner.

Homeowners sometime believe that their beloved second home will be used, abused and destroyed by vacation renters, so they definitely don't want to put good furnishings or anything of value in the home.

Here's what Alex Risser, owner of Outer Beaches Realty in Avon, North Carolina and former President of the Vacation Rental Managers Association, has to say about this:

- *"The good news with that is you only have an exposure of 7 days at a time whereas with a long term rental, you may not even see the property until a year later and who knows what's happened during that time. So it's kind of good because you only have a very short time period where if you have somebody who's not taken care of the property that they can potentially cause damage. But for the most part vacation renters are terrific people. **They are you and me on vacation**.*

- *We have a certain code of ethics and responsibility in our lives and that doesn't change when we go to rent a vacation home. We are still sensitive to other people's property and we want to take care of something. So the incidence of having a nightmare tenant in a vacation home is really pretty low. The experience base of professional property managers would verify that – that it's a very low incident rate."*

And I love the way Leigh Clarke, Managing Director of Railey Mountain Lake Rentals puts it.

- *"Ok, I would say the most common misconception would be that it's just a rental so you never want to put anything nice into it. And I like to tell people that when you take your family and your little kids to the (low cost budget) hotel, you tell them to sleep in the bed with their shoes on...*

- *But when you go to the Four Seasons you make everyone take their shoes off at the door of the room because you're much more meticulous about how you care for it and as a normal human being that's how you behave."*

Couldn't have said it better myself, Leigh!

VACATION RENTAL HOMES ARE JUST NOT TOP GRADE CONTENDERS

Some people believe this myth. There is a misconception that vacation rentals are not nice properties to begin with, that they are run down, not cared for and they are not an advantage to a town. While there are some properties like this, it is definitely not the rule anymore. It may have been more prevalent in the past, I don't really know, but the average rental today, if it is going to attract guests, must have all the amenities of home. In fact, the places which offer more amenities and quality furnishings rent better and demand more money. Most of us in the business, feel that the nicer and more upscale the property, the more it will be respected by the guest. It doesn't hurt that there will also be more opportunity to rent it and for larger amounts of money. It is not unusual for properties to rent from $5,000 to $15,000 per week. That is a substantial amount of money and people expect and deserve a great deal when they are paying these sums.

CHAPTER 3

TIME: THE RENTAL CLOCK IS TICKING

Bad Timing!

One of the busiest weeks of the summer, mid July, we had a husband, wife and their 4 children, dog, packed car, etc, show up to check into their rental property. The only problem is that we did not have them listed anywhere!

They were all exhausted from a long ride, so we sent them to a local restaurant where they could eat and cool off. We scurried around while they were gone and indeed we found a reservation for them – for mid August, not mid July. We showed them all the correspondence we had had with them, the signed contracts, and the wife looked at her cell phone's calendar and found the date noted in mid August.

We were able to avert disaster, however, by getting the owner of their property rental for August to release money paid to them. We then placed the family in an open cottage for the current week. We received a wonderful gift basket for all our staff from a very grateful family who return every year.

Seaside Vacation Rentals
York, Maine

TIME:
THE RENTAL CLOCK IS TICKING

TICK TOCK...

Ok, I know you are saying, "Time seems too simple a concept to devote to an entire chapter". Yet I think it is perhaps the single most important element for you, as a homeowner to consider in choosing whether to rent your vacation home yourself or to go with choose a professional agency. Time is an inherent factor in every step of the renting process and as an owner, you need to gage gauge whether or not you are willing to devote the amount of time necessary to accomplish successful renting, this includes the care of your property. What is the value of your time?

No matter what you normally earn, even if you pay yourself minimum wage, you should determine what time you'll need to expend and what your time is worth.

GETTING THE RIGHT GAME VENUE

This?

Or this?

At the onset, your time involved will include choosing the right property with the intention of renting. You need to be prepared prior to your purchase, or if you already own a property, to find out what it will take to make it most rentable. This can include furnishings, repairs, and regional market differences in what precise things are expected at a property. For instance, are linens included? Will you contract the service or take care of doing the laundry service yourself between guests? What rental price range does the property fall in? And please try to be completely honest with yourselves about the difficulty of renting when there is an emotional attachment to a property. Finding the right property can take days, months and in some cases, years!

PREPARATION AND TRAINING

Time is a huge factor in preparing the property to be rented. At the very, very beginning you'll need to get well taken, attractive photographs of the property, compose an accurate yet appealing listing description and choose a vehicle on the web in which to market the property.

What other means are you going to use for marketing? The amount of time and research to find and choose the correct avenues to market your property can be significant. Once you have determined all factors and have gotten everything online, then we need to talk about time in a whole different way.

DEADLINES

Let's look at time devoted to responding to inquiries and keeping an accurate calendar. *It is essential, not only to respond to inquires for specific dates, but to accurately and quickly reply to people so that they will not move on to another property.* Moving on is exactly what they will do because there are so many alternatives available to them at any one time. Vacation home renting is done very much like hotel renting, in that you would not want to wait a week or even days to hear back from a potential choice if you are a guest looking for a property. You want instantaneous response or pretty close to it. Then add the time element for simply answering questions on the property. Does your website offer the ability for the guests to share the property listing with others in their party by emailing brochures?

VIEWING THE PROPERTY

Some people may expect to actually see the property which means that you have to include the time that you have to travel to get to the property and show your place to prospective renters. That time may or may not be rewarded by an actual reservation.

The other key element that vacation rental managers sometimes find is that when people do insist on seeing a property, very frequently the callers do not even show up, so your time may have been completely in vain. But let's assume that you get a reservation from them.

CONTRACTS AND RED TAPE

The next time element involved is finding and preparing a good contract between you and the guest. Please don't use a form you find at your local office supply store. It isn't designed for vacation rentals.

You'll also need to collect a reasonable amount of money to ensure that the guest will not walk away from the reservation. You'll need to decide on a cancellation policy which should be very obviously and accurately stated in your contract with the guest.

GETTING PAID

And here's the whole point of what your doing - getting paid! Collecting the money can be a difficult and time consuming part of the transaction. Are you going to take only cash and checks? Or will you take credit cards? Very often in a personal transaction people may be willing to send a check, but if you are only going to take checks or cash then you will need to consider the time you are waiting to receive your money and for checks to clear that the property would be off the market. If that renter doesn't send the money within a week or so, then you need to get in touch with them and begin a process of perhaps allowing them additional time if they seem to have a good reason as to why they have not sent the money.

Then you may decide to take the property off the market for an additional length of time for them. And while this doesn't seem like a big deal, there is a very tight rental season for most places in which people will book your property. After a certain point, your property, no matter how desirable, may not get rented, due to that small window of time when people will actually book the property. So that's another time factor to consider.

FORGET BARTERING... DON'T PLAY GAMES WITH YOUR MONEY

Just as an aside, over the years, people have asked me about exchanging homes in different areas for no cost. If you don't know the other party you would exchange with, *why* would you want to do this? You don't know what you'll get, who is in your house, and you won't get paid.

And especially as an agency with our entire overhead, why would we choose not to get paid or get some token amount? Another frequent question has been whether or not we have any paid house-sitting jobs. That may be prevalent somewhere, but I've never seen it and why would an agency want to be involved?

OK, YOU CAN PLAY WITH CREDIT CARDS, TOO

And if you look at methods of payments other than check or cash, you'll need to take the time to set up an account with a credit card processing company. Some of the websites that cater to homeowners who are renting their properties themselves do offer this service, and of course, there is a charge for that so you'll need to consider the cost of that as it will come out of your profits.

THE 'IRS' DOESN'T PLAY GAMES

So let's assume renting your place by yourself has gone well. By the way, did you ever collect the balance of money due... and how much time did you have to invest in collecting it? Another extremely important element is to find out if your state, region or town, has a tax on renting. If so, you'll need to register to pay that tax. And remember to report the tax. I urge you very strongly, to know the tax requirements and adhere strictly to them.

You must report your income and pay the taxes on your rentals. Most states and regions are looking for people who don't pay and the fines can be significant. Taking care of the tax filing is very time consuming. Just think of filing your taxes at the end of the year when you do your income taxes. Granted, filing monthly taxes doesn't take anywhere near as much time but it is meticulous and it does have to be done not only accurately but in a timely manner.

And if you're in a region in which you have a state tax, a regional tax, a town tax, you may even have other types of taxes to pay - they all need to go to different sources. So you might have that tax reporting issue multiplied a number of times. Even agencies that do it all the time will run into times with the tax authorities when there are questions. The tax folks may ask whether this guest paid the full amount, or the tax office didn't receive their check on time or that they don't have the records for something. (Yes, the state does lose stuff.)

All I can say is that time is an amazingly huge factor. It sounds like it shouldn't be much but I think if you ask an agency or someone who has done a great deal of renting on their own, you'll find that, yes, this is a real pain.

If you don't have scrupulous record keeping of every month, every reservation, every payment of money that you've collected and copies of checks, et cetera, you will eat up more of your time with bureaucratic follow up for questions the authorities have or even mistakes they have made. Tax reporting is thus another area that in which we frequently underestimate the amount of time that this type of renting involves.

So that's the money factor and we now are assuming that you've got the money for the reservation and the booking has been confirmed.

PROMOTING YOUR PROPERTY

Let's move on to the time element involved with renting slow weeks or off season. There are instances where you have rented a portion of the time you have available, but not all. How do you stimulate people to rent the remaining weeks? What kind of incentives do you offer? Are you going to lower the price? Do you offer giveaways or incentives that might entice people to choose those less desirable weeks?

You need to put the time and effort into marketing in a different way to promote renting off season. You could choose to work with an event, perhaps be a sponsor in promoting it. You could also offer something like a two night free stay as part of a raffle for an off season event that might stimulate people to look at your property. Very often however, major community organizations doing events don't want to work with an individual owner that way, they prefer to work with a professional business. There are ways in which you can do it, however. Again the major element is time, how much time do you have to devote to this.

CLEAN UP, WILL YOU

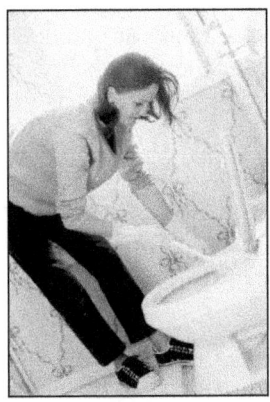

Ok, now let's say you've got the majority of your weeks rented and you are happily heading into the prime season. One major thing that many homeowners do not devote enough time to, even when they work with a professional agency, is to thoroughly spring clean their property. This is such a crucial thing. Spring cleaning a property takes days, not hours. This is something that really must be done prior to a heavy renting season because the minor cleaning issues will only be exacerbated once that property has multiple families using it. Spring cleaning is certainly not a pleasant job and is very time consuming.

Many professional agencies run into the issue of homeowners who do not want to spend the time or money to do a spring cleaning or don't understand the importance of it. In my own particular company we are frequently assured that this service has been done and we will begin the season with the first renter reporting major complaints. Then we have to send a cleaning crew out to the house to do what can only be a marginal job because there are people in there already.

Plus, to then satisfy the person vacationing there, we may need to give money back, and that's going to hurt you, the homeowner. In worst case scenarios it can even mean moving a guest to another property because they are so dissatisfied.

It's easy to think, "Hey, I left the property clean and neat last fall and everything was perfect when I closed the property down". But the bottom line is that any inactive property that's been closed for months or had a long term renter in there is going to need some serious attention. The amount of time needed to clean is crucial to running this business - and this is a business if you're renting.

NO, I MEAN <u>REALLY</u> CLEAN

So you've got the property spring cleaned which took days, and everything is just the way you want it to be. Have you, if you are renting the property yourself, set up a cleaning person or will you perhaps come in whenever there is a break in the guest calendar to clean the property again?

This regular cleaning, if one person is doing it, can be anywhere from a two to four hour job depending on the size of the house and the amenities in the property. We have had homeowners who insisted on doing their own cleaning, which I frankly think is just a little crazy if you are working with a professional agency.

Yes, cleaning services could cost you some money (although, in some cases the guest pays for cleaning), but you may feel you need to be more involved with how it's cleaned.

I think it is a poor choice of a homeowner's time to drive two to three hours to get to their property, spend several hours cleaning and then drive home through heavy Saturday traffic.

I NEED A TOWEL

Now, have you considered if linens (sheets and towels) are expected in your region of the country and if you are supplying those? If so, you should have a laundry system that clearly meets health standards which require linens be laundered at 120 degree minimum water temperature which most residential laundry setups do not have. You want to have a system for monitoring your linens. You'll need enough stock to rotate them so that you do not have to wait for one setup to be dried to make the bed. What if a sheet or pillowcase goes missing? You'll need enough linen to handle multiple turnovers.

FINER POINTS OF THE GAME

Ok so we've got the linens, we've got the cleaning done; now you need to handle the check-ins. How are you planning to transfer the property keys to your guests?

Please don't tell me you are going to leave the key under a flower pot in front of the house. That would be a real mistake because of the obvious security reasons but also because no one is meeting and greeting those people who are coming into your property and that to me is a loss for you from a marketing outlook, and from a security standpoint.

You should have concerns about limits on the number of people allowed, whether there are pets, do they smoke. There will be a number of things that are important to you and by meeting the guests you are now a real live person to them, not just an email or voice on the phone. As well, your guests are now real people with real expectations.

However, if you are going to meet the guest at the property or elsewhere, your lecture or long list of no-no's to an incoming guest may not be appreciated. Basically, that is the kiss of death! One of the benefits of working with an agency is they have had multiple contacts with the group that's renting your property. Many agencies insist on a person to person check in where a guest is handed the keys, then the keys are monitored and returned to that agency, plus noted that they have been returned and they have a safe setup for late arrivals. That way, for the purposes of security, you do not have somebody arriving late at night in the dark and finding that either the key that was under the flower pot is not where it's supposed to be or that the house has been left unlocked and the keys are inside.

Frankly, if I were that guest coming in from an urban environment or anywhere and found that kind of a situation, it would really frighten me. I think a great many people feel very uncomfortable about that. There are some remote locations where meeting a guest is just not possible, but measures should still be taken to ensure security. Many agencies utilize remote lock systems or lockboxes. That is just another factor of the check in process to consider.

RENTAL INFORMATION

You need to get the information to guests that they will need for the week. Give them explicit directions to get there. What day trash is picked up and where?

Are there any idiosyncrasies about the property that they need to know in order to have a comfortable and happy time there? What is the wireless password?

Moving forward, the guest has had a good time, and then they leave. Where do they leave the key? Where do they check out? There's that key issue again, but you have that handled.

EMERGENCIES (EVERY GAME GETS RAINED OUT SOMETIMES)

Most agencies have some sort of reporting mechanism if something goes wrong while the guest is there... even brand new houses have things go wrong. The hot water heater doesn't work or the toilet gets plugged, you know... something fun like that! I can guarantee you it will happen when you least want it to happen. You'll get a call at 11:30pm on a Saturday night and something has gone wrong. Are you going to jump in your car and try to handle that problem? Do you have the skills to handle that problem? Are you going to call a repair person or a professional to take care of it? And if you do, do you have a relationship with that person so that they are going to get up in the middle of the night and do it for you?

In some cases, professionals like septic pumping companies, plumbers and electricians will only do a job like this in the middle of the night if they receive a check then and there. And you will be charged a huge amount of money, but hey, if you can get it done that's ok.

The advantage for agencies is that they have so many different properties, very often professional trades people are trying to get on their call list because there is so much work generated from the agencies.

Plus the management company is hopefully professional and has a good reputation. If they are paying trades people on a timely basis, the pros will take care of whatever needs to be done.

As well, many agencies have maintenance staff that can take care of most problems and an emergency call service is often available to guests.

ARE YOU PREPARED FOR THE COMPETITION?

Even before the high season you look at your property and evaluate it. You might say, "Ok, I really need to repaint. The house has had a lot of use last summer and I've made 'x' amount of dollars. If I look at this as a business then I really need to put maybe ten percent back into the property. Maybe I will upgrade the bedding, the furniture, we need a new set of dishes, or we need to repaint the deck in the spring." You need to make the decision as a homeowner if you are personally going to do the work. Again, that is an enormous time factor.

And if you want to upgrade the dishes, or the comforters or the bedding, you have to factor in the shopping time for those items and choosing good working colors. That sounds superficial, doesn't it, but colors are important. I've had homeowners who had pure white bedroom sets in a high family use setting. It looks beautiful the first time you see it, but it's immensely impractical from the standpoint of families renting the property.

I frequently end up recommending that they put it all away and purchase something different. Had they approached me before they made their purchases, they wouldn't be in the position of having colors or fabrics that basically just don't work at all.

Purchasing items for your second home is important and sometimes fun; I just want to make sure each homeowner is aware of the amount of time involved with so many of these things.

GEARING UP FOR NEXT SEASON

You've gotten through the season, you repainted, and you've closed it up for the off season. Have you received a commitment from your guests who rented last summer wanting to return next summer? You need to know when you have to start the process again.

A property is truly successful when it has a large number of re-rentals. Once a property starts to get and retain repeat renters, it's a good situation for both the guests and the homeowner because the same people are coming back year after year.

So then there are many less weeks that you have to worry about trying to rent. However, if you're not getting commitments for those re-rentals that should be telling you something: 1) that the price is too high, 2) the property was not as they had expected, or 3) the guest felt that their needs were not met. These three items comprise almost universally what the problem is if the property is not getting re-rentals.

TAX REPORTING, SOME FOLKS TAKE ALL THE FUN OUT OF THE GAME

At the end of the year, you have to file your taxes, which of course you do; but be sure you have all your records in place. Gross rental income, what exactly you spent on the property. What can be deducted, what can't? Get it all together and bring it to your tax accountant.

Most professional agencies will provide you with a 1099 form and a statement that breaks down gross income and agency expenses such as commission, maintenance or cleaning.

Any additional personal expenses made for the property would not be included, but it certainly takes care of the bulk of things.

REVIEWING GAME STRATEGIES

The time factor in evaluating whether to handle rentals yourself or use an agency, as I said in the beginning, seems deceptively simple but is truly a major factor. Anyone going into vacation renting is starting a new business. Can you commit to that? This chapter hopes to bring about a realization of how much time is involved and evaluating what your time is worth.

If you look at it objectively and hired somebody else to do these things, what would you be willing to compensate that person for doing it? Even at minimum wage, the amount of time involved far exceeds what you might pay a professional agency. I do feel that time is probably the most critical element in making a decision whether to go with a professional agency or to rent your vacation home yourself.

CHAPTER 4

EDUCATION & TRAINING: THE GAME TAKES SKILL

Bats in the Belfry

One summer, while we were renting a huge old summer cottage located on the ocean, we received a call from the guest that she had seen a bat. She was terrified! We sent over one of our maintenance guys who was working for us during his summer college break. There was indeed a bat! It had adhered itself to a window and I think the bat was even more terrified than the guest. Our guy, Kevin, brought it to the local wildlife center. But the story doesn't end there. The guest was absolutely sure that the bat was rabid and that she was going to get rabies.

We called the state capitol and were put in touch with a doctor who worked with rabies control. We asked if he would speak to our guest on speaker phone. She was just about hysterical by this point and asked if she could have contracted rabies if the bat had flown overhead during the night while she was asleep. (The bat hadn't actually come anywhere near her, let alone bit her.)

The doctor was very sweet at first, but after numerous times of reassuring her that she could not have contracted rabies, he finally told the guest that the only way she could have contracted rabies in the manner she was describing, is if she had an open gaping wound and the bat fell into it!

Seaside Vacation Rentals
York, Maine

EDUCATION AND TRAINING: THIS GAME TAKES SKILL

The education and training of vacation rental managers varies dramatically. There are no college degrees or certifications in universities for vacation rental professionals, unfortunately. The Vacation Rental Managers Association (VRMA) has begun a process of certification for professionals with a set of courses that are critical to the professional in this field. However, this program is recent and very few people have actually completed those certifications. Looking to the future, however, it should be a real asset.

WHAT SKILLS TO LOOK FOR IN AN AGENCY

Now this sounds very roundabout and I know that the title of this chapter is education and training and it is not a misnomer. The education and training of vacation rental pros simply comes about in a variety of ways and yes, roundabout ways. It's not a straight line from entering college and majoring in vacation rental management, that's not a possibility. So I am going to give you a couple of case studies of different people who've been successful in the business and their backgrounds, Hopefully, you'll see that their skill set, their education and training in a variety of interrelated fields make them ideally suited to do this business.

VARIETY PLAYS WELL IN THIS ARENA

The most surprising thing about the educational background and training of vacation rental professionals is that they come from such an amazingly varied background.

I interviewed many vacation rental managers currently in the industry, and one of the questions I asked is how they ended up in this business.

There were no two answers alike. There was Cort Roussel at Franconia Notch Reservations who was selling ski lift tickets and was recruited by a very perceptive vacation rental manager, Jim Collier, former President of Loon Reservation Services in Lincoln, NH. Jim saw Cort's potential and ten years later Cort Roussel bought a branch office of the business from Jim, his mentor. Currently, Cort is a very successful vacation rental business owner in the White Mountains area of New Hampshire.

Another interesting example is Steve Trover, President of the Vacation Rental Managers Association and All Star Vacation Homes in Kissimmee Florida, who was exporting cars overseas.

Audrey Miller, President of The Cottage Connection in Boothbay, Maine, was working in a Silicon Valley Think Tank and her husband, Jeff, was a Captain on a boat in Boothbay when she returned home there. They started a successful company doing vacation rentals.

INTERESTING CONTENDERS

Some others have excellent business, MBA type backgrounds. There are also a variety of educational backgrounds prominent with people who've started in the business. Many vacation rental management businesses are Mom and Pop operations run by a husband and wife or a family group who may have had no prior experience in the industry before going into this business.

So, as a homeowner, you might ask this author how that equates to education and training. The answer is that the proof of their education and training is evident in their success and survival in the business.

Knowing how many years they have been at it and what kind of reputation they have in the community will tell you whether they run a good operation or not. Inspecting their marketing materials and contractual information as well as asking other homeowners for their feedback, will give you a good sense of how well they are equipped to handle being a vacation rental manager.

Another key question to ask is if they are members of organizations which provide ongoing training in business and marketing, as well as vacation rental specific tools. Are they members of, for instance, chambers of commerce and perhaps networking groups; or have they taken courses or have a degree in business? What is their prior work history and how does it relate to the vacation rental management industry.

DO THEY WORK WELL AS A TEAM?

One of the key factors involved with choosing your vacation rental company will be to look at the interaction between the staff and the owner/leader of that company. Does the staff respect the company management? Does the staff feel they are heard by management? Perhaps the best education any rental vacation manager can have is to simply listen to their staff as they evaluate potential problems and solutions that make a business run more smoothly, more effectively and grow successfully.

TOURISM PLAYS A PART

Another background that can be instrumental in the success of a vacation rental manager is the hotel and restaurant industry. Many vacation rental management people come from a hospitality background, and that is no accident. Hotels and restaurants lean heavily towards customer service and operating efficiency. The skills crucial to running a successful vacation rental management company can easily be born in this environment.

REAL ESTATE AGENTS KNOW LOTS OF MOVES, TOO

In some states, vacation rental management falls under the real estate commission. In the states that do require it, the manager must take a certain number of real estate courses every year and is provided with legal and other real estate information that can be very helpful to them. Also, if they are members of Realtors, they have to take ethics courses and learn the proper way to handle money with a trust account. That is definitely desirable.

States that don't have vacation rental professionals under the umbrella of the real estate commission still get the education that they need. Vacation rental managers in those states often do have real estate licenses and the same education as well.

Vacation rental managers may also have a real estate arm of their business. In wearing their second hat as a realtor they get the educational courses. There is a very strong debate as to whether vacation rental managers should fall under the auspices of real estate commissions, and in another chapter of this book, we'll discuss the pros and cons.

But for now, let's just say there are definitely advantages and disadvantages on both sides. Just know that there are courses required through real estate and that they can provide additional education.

THE MORE YOUR AGENCY KNOWS, THE MORE YOUR TEAM WINS!

I think that the best rental professional is someone who avails himself of training opportunities wherever he can. But beyond the manager of a vacation rental agency, it's extremely important that the staff get as much education as possible. When contemplating an agency, find out if the staff receives customer service education. Is staff well trained in using the software? What are the staff training periods and does staff have the tools to handle things when they arise? This is something that is not easy to ask a vacation rental manager. However, it is usually apparent when you deal with them whether or not the staff has had the advantages of ongoing training.

One of the things that Seaside does with our staff is to host two annual events. First, in the fall of every year, we close the office for a day and have a 'Think Tank' to review the season. We question what went right and what went wrong and how we can make it work more efficiently. Everyone has a say about each department. The only rule is that it is not a complaint session so if you have a problem, you have to offer a solution. Lastly, we always have a theme which no one knows in advance.

The other event is held just after the start of the New Year and it is 'Kickoff'. In the Kickoff session, we unveil our plan for the upcoming year, incorporating the best of the ideas from the 'Think Tank' session. Kickoff also has a theme that no one knows before arrival.

Here are some photos from past Think Tanks and Kickoff meetings.

Themes have included Oscar Night, CSI, Mardi Gras, World Traveler, Star Wars and my favorite, our most recent, Monopoly played with our properties.

As you can see, we have a lot of fun with these events, but we also gain a lot of knowledge and our staff has helped to make us real contenders in our vacation rental market.

The other important factor to consider with training is finding out if an agency cooperates with their competitors and other businesses in the community. Do they network throughout their region and even nationally? Networking itself provides a tremendous amount of mentoring, as well as cutting edge information for managers and staff.

Some of Seaside's amazing crew!

WHO SHARES THE GAME PLAN?

Some really good insights that I have gained were from Stewart Couch, owner of Hatteras Realty, with whom I served on the Board of Directors of the Vacation Rental Managers Association.

My crew and I even vacationed in Cape Hatteras and he was immensely welcoming. He has since passed away, and is a great loss to the industry.

**Margaret Regan, Kyle Beal, Lillian McDonald,
Robin Hansen, Cape Hatteras, NC**

As well as networking, the increased contact between agencies gives the vacation rental manager and staff ways of connecting with and asking questions of others if they run into something later that they've not dealt with before and are not sure how to handle. Communication is something that can only make the industry stronger and better all around.

BRING IN A PROFESSIONAL TRAINER

Smart agencies often invest in hiring a consultant to review their overall operations or to address a particular need.

- *"(One) benefit of a consultant is that the consultant helps you set goals; like hiring a personal trainer vs. going to the gym yourself. Someone to make a roadmap to excellence."*

Doug Kennedy, President
Kennedy Training Network
Hollywood, FL

This can reap huge rewards for the agency, the homeowner, and the guest. A consulting firm with knowledge of the vacation rental business can be an agency's best investment.

"Seaside Vacation Rentals, hired a consultant a while ago to see how customer service oriented our staff was, how many of our staff were actually closing on reservation calls, and to add to our training. It was interesting to learn that the people we thought would ace this, did not. We were surprised at some of the staff who did very well at reservations and customer service! We learned not to make assumptions and we also learned that hiring a good consultant could actually make us better and earn more money for our owners."

Jennifer Thibodeau, COO
Seaside Vacation Rentals
York, Maine

(Agencies may want to check our website, **www.the-rental-game.com**, for consulting information and links to a number of great firms.)

WHAT RULES YOUR AGENCY <u>MUST</u> KNOW TO STAY IN THE GAME

Vacation rental pros must have knowledge about state and federal laws governing rentals.

This can be quite involved since it depends how the state views vacation rentals. Vacation rentals may fall under real estate. They may fall under landlord/tenant law or they may fall under hotel and/or transient stay state laws. Homeowners would not be expected to have that particular knowledge that could turn out to be a huge detriment to them.

For example, the collection and return of security deposits are tightly controlled under these laws. In southern Maine, we offer longer term rentals. When a homeowner wants the extra income and/or wants their home occupied during the long winter months, we will rent this property as a winter rental. Typically, these run along the dates of the school year.

However, just one item in winter renting to note, a security deposit at the end of a lease must be returned within a certain number of days (30) or the owner of the property may be liable for double that amount as a penalty in Maine. As you can see, the results could be extremely painful for a homeowner who does this incorrectly.

MORE RULES?? YOU BET!

There are a lot of details involved, even in this instance that affect the security deposit. Were there damages? If so, a written estimate of those damages must be sent to the tenant and extends those thirty days. How does a homeowner have access to this knowledge?

What if somebody refused to leave a property that they were renting for a week? In some states, eviction could actually fall under traditional landlord/tenant laws in which eviction could take six to eight months!

Fortunately, in thirty years, I have never run across this. I emphasize it only to point out that you really need to know what you are getting into before you decide to rent your property yourself. This could be devastating to a homeowner.

DID I MENTION THE RULES CAN CHANGE?

Vacation rental managers need to have knowledge of the trends in the industry. For instance, in the past, most guests looking to rent a vacation home used to rent six months to a year prior to the dates of their vacation. That is no longer true. With the internet and pressure by television and other media, most vacationers are waiting close to the last minute to get good deals. This trend has definitely impacted the vacation rental industry; therefore bookings are coming in closer and closer to the actual beginning of a vacation rental.

WHAT IS WINNING?

Knowing the trends in the industry can make one rental agency successful over another. Amenities like having internet or Wi-Fi in the home are now a top request. Of course, trends vary from region to region. For example, in some areas vacation rentals cater to singles, couples or young professionals, in other areas they draw families. In still other areas family reunions are the big draw with large multi generational groups. Some areas do a lot of corporate business retreats. Additionally, there are some areas with events such as weddings, reunions or as we like to say in the vacation rental industry, the SMERF factor, which is Social, Military, Educational, Religious and Fraternal. The acronym covers get-togethers in any of those areas.

WHO WANTS TO PLAY?

Whether you are renting your place yourself or working with a rental manager, knowledge of trends is very important. That wisdom certainly helps in knowing where to market, which to market to, how to price things and what people are looking for.

If it's a corporate rental, a lot more business tools need to be available, meeting space size is a consideration, and maybe audio visual equipment.

At Seaside, we have had groups of women who getaway in the fall, just for a girls' get together. We have older women that rent vacation rental properties to do quilting, scrapbooking and any number of things. It's a lot of fun and a great way for friends to meet and have time together.

I would also like to note that more education is available to the vacation rental companies than to individuals. Because agencies are in the business, there is always a webinar on one thing or another or a vendor who may have a white paper on certain statistical research. So in this process the manager learns what is cutting edge and what is happening in the industry and related businesses.

PUT SOME MONEY ON IT

One of the key factors that education and training help with is the ability to price your property correctly. Agencies are able to come up with a price that should get it booked through researching comparable properties for rent and those that have rented. And they can help you, the homeowner, to equip your house in a fashion that will make it enticing for guests to rent and get you the best price.

As a homeowner, you have the ability to see what is out there for rent, but frequently can't find what has rented and at what price. This is a major flaw. It has a lot in common with trying to sell your own home.

You can see what is for sale out there and what is being asked for properties that are similar to yours, but do you know which of these properties has actually sold within the last six months, and at what price? That is the crucial element in pricing your house to sell.

When we talk about renting, some people may say, "Well, I just look at the other property's calendar on a 'rent by owner' website and I can see it is completely booked at this crazy price." But is it really booked, or is blocked for owner time with their family.

So your knowledge of what weeks the place has actually rented and for what price is limited. Yes, you may be able to get information from a neighbor or other people that have similar properties, but there is always the possibility that the neighbor will either downplay the amount of money or time rented or pump it up a little bit to make themselves feel better.

CHAPTER 5

HOSPITALITY & CUSTOMER SERVICE: IT'S NOT JUST WINNING, IT'S HOW YOU PLAY

Golfers' Handicap

One of the best and most appalling stories I have ever heard came from Billy Bernier, who runs the Brunswick Plantation Resort and Golf Course in Calabash, NC, not far from Myrtle Beach. Well, Billy had these four guys who were truly avid golfers who came every year for a week in the spring. Nothing, or almost nothing, interfered with their tee times. So Billy was greatly surprised one morning when two of the guys came into the office and said there would only be the two of them playing that morning. When Billy asked why, one of them replied, "because Charlie died last night and Sam drew the short straw to drive him back to Ohio." Billy said, "You're kidding, right?" "No", the guy responded, "take a look right out there in the car." Sure enough, there was Sam behind the wheel and Charlie, dead, in the passenger seat.

Needless to say there was a lot of discussion among Billy's staff as to how Sam would explain things if they got pulled over for speeding.

Billy Bernier, Resort Director
Brunswick Plantation Resort, Calabash, NC

HOSPITALITY & CUSTOMER SERVICE: IT'S NOT JUST ABOUT WINNING, IT'S HOW YOU PLAY

Hospitality and customer service are key to the vacation rental experience, however the individual homeowner may or may not have had training in these areas. For that matter, the professional vacation rental professional may not either, but, the vacation rental pro will have to get very good at this quickly, or fail in his business.

WHO IS THE COACH

When it comes to customer service and hospitality with your property, a vacation rental manager is just more objective. Understandably, being objective is often a very difficult thing for you, as the homeowner; to accomplish - especially when there may be a problem with your property that you don't feel should be a reason for a complaint.

REFEREES HANDLE COMPLAINTS ALL THE TIME

A complaint is something that has to be handled with a great deal of diplomacy and a good professional vacation rental manager can act as a buffer between homeowner and guest. They may be able to at least understand the situation, especially if you feel attacked by a guest reporting a complaint. It is very difficult to look at your own wonderful property, knowing that you've worked so hard on it and here is somebody staying there for a week and complaining about something insignificant. The guest may be very upset. For instance, there is no Wi-Fi available for their laptop. They just can't believe that you would have a house without wifi and they may complain about the décor, they may complain about the size of the rooms, the amenities, and many, many, many things which may feel irrelevant or even hurtful to a homeowner who loves their house.

Steve Zimmerman, owner of Beach House Logos in Pittstown, NJ, and a vacation homeowner as well, said,

- *"We got a call from a homeowner last night who was looking to buy some sweatshirts as a gift for their guests and she's a VRBO (Vacation Rental by Owner). So I started asking her why she did one (rent herself) versus the other (use a manager) and it was a pretty interesting story. I guess it comes down to a few basic things which are: how heavily involved do you want to get into something; and how fast can you handle whatever situation comes out of it. So we talked a little bit about that yesterday because she was doing everything on her own. I said I never have because I just don't want to deal with the headaches. So it really comes down to, I guess, a basic fundamental feeling between, let's say this woman I was talking to, and myself as to what you feel capable of handling yourself.*

- *And she said, she'd had relatively few incidents so far, but I don't think she has ever had to deal with a situation like a couple weeks ago. We thought we had a water leak in the house and it turned out we had termites. So in our case if we didn't have someone able to turn this around and fix it as quickly as possible we could have potentially lost a couple weeks of rental income."*

DEFENSE?

Often you, as a homeowner, feel that everyone else should value your house the way you do. There must be something wrong with that guest who doesn't appreciate it. (And who knows, there may be...) The fact of the matter is that everyone is different and people expect different things from their experience.

We learned long ago that the guests' expectations may seem unimportant to us, but to them they can mean the difference between a vacation that is a success and a miserable vacation. If they don't get exactly what they expect and frequently unfulfilled expectations are heightened by things like a week of rain, or they couldn't get to the beach or they've had an argument with their partner or a million other things that really have nothing to do with the home. That's when it's good to have somebody that can calm things down and be rational and reasonable with that guest and with the homeowner and come to an agreeable solution.

As far as the training part of it goes, many times vacation rental managers don't have any more experience than the average homeowner, but as I said before, they do have a little more objectivity because it is not their property and they have no emotional tie to it.

NOT SO OFFENSIVE

Very frequently, though, people in the vacation rental industry do have some sort of customer service background. It isn't always something directly in vacation rentals; they may have worked in hotels or restaurants or in strong tourism areas. They have a pretty fair idea of what is expected of them when it comes to guests and certainly they learn very, very quickly when they have to deal with this.

Also, there are many organizations in the tourism industry that offer training in customer service relations and this training is utilized by many vacation rental companies. Networking and finding out how other agencies have solved certain problems allows an agency to become proficient in the skills needed to run a good business as well.

THE MEDIATOR

The ability to offer customer service and hospitality is not unique to the vacation rental professional. Any homeowner who wishes to rent their property themselves can do this, however it is more difficult because it is their home and that attachment weakens their ability to be open to criticism. The other difficult part is that often when there is a complaint there is a need to either give back a portion of the money that they have received, or offer something of value to the person who has the complaint. The vacation rental manager can do that. They know that there are going to be any number of warranted or unwarranted complaints across the summer, in some cases they may have made arrangements with other businesses in the area to perhaps offer a gift certificate or a dinner out.

The professional understands that the guest may have gone without a particular service or amenity and the vacation rental manager is able to put a value on the loss. The pro deals with these things on a more frequent basis than an individual homeowner and has consulted with other agencies to get a feel for how to adequately compensate the person with the complaint.

EXTRA POINTS

Another important feature to customer service and hospitality is a very good knowledge of the area where the vacation home is located and the ability to connect guests to services, attractions and restaurants. The vacation rental manager in these cases acts as a concierge by advising the guest where to find a place to get their nails done, go to a spa, find good shopping, or an out of the way restaurant that specializes in a certain cuisine. The agency may even offer discounts to some of these places. While the homeowner may have a certain amount of that knowledge too, they may not have as much local knowledge or know the out of way places. Nor does a guest always feel comfortable calling an owner for area information. As the homeowner, you may not have connections with area businesses and to be able to arrange lunch or a gift certificate for a guest who is unable to check in on time because your property was not ready.

The vacation rental professional can just call the restaurant's owner, because they know them, and say "look, I'll come by tomorrow and take care of this. Please just give them whatever they want and we'll pay for it". This can sometimes work as well as giving back a larger sum of money for a problem. Of course, it differs with each complaint.

Knowing how to turn down a ridiculous demand for compensation is a part of vacation renting, too.

Several years ago, two burners on a stovetop could not be replaced during the week the "Jones" stayed. They demanded their entire vacation for free, plus wanted an oceanfront place for the following year for free, too, as compensation. We did reimburse them a small amount and gave them dinner out. We also wrote a note letting them know that was the total of their reimbursement.

The agency also has an active referral list for maintenance professionals in the area. Generally, a homeowner would not have as comprehensive a list of people that they can get to quickly. The vacation rental manager has established business relationships. Such relationships compel area plumbers or electricians to go out of their way especially on nights or weekends to take care of an issue at a property for that agency.

In my estimation, the response to a problem when it occurs is the true measure of customer service.

Hospitality has to do with how a guest is greeted and every step of the vacation rental process before that person even arrives. Once the guest has arrived, making sure that the rental group is having a good vacation.

A quick phone call from the staff to ask, "Is everything ok?" allows an agency to react quickly to issues that may have occurred and it's great when they can be corrected by the vacation rental professional early in the week. We don't want it to become a huge factor for guests. Very often a small thing can build if it isn't addressed, as we all know.

A WINNING SEASON

Hospitality and customer service even extend beyond the end of a reservation.

The guest and homeowner have knowledge and information that a successful vacation rental manager will want to use as part of their business growth and learning. They can do this by actively seeking information from the guest as they leave through surveys or other means of contact. The owners need to be apprised of the results of those surveys in order to keep their property well maintained and on the cutting edge of what guests want.

The homeowner's input should be sought as well. What do they need and what are they looking for from the vacation rental manager and what is important to them for their home and for their guests?

Peter Wenk of Virtual Resort Manager in Beaufort, NC, says,

- *"Basically, when you hire a rental agent you're establishing a relationship. In any business it's a one on one relationship and you want that relationship to be compatible and know that you're comfortable with the person that you chose to rent your property."*

I think the main thing with customer service and hospitality is that everyone wants to be treated as unique and special, everyone wants to be heard. If they had a problem and were responded to quickly and respectfully, they'll appreciate it. As I said earlier, it is certainly something that a homeowner can do themselves, however it is more difficult to do when it's your own property. Very often it's easy to have a very minor situation escalate by being defensive about a complaint or problem.

CHAPTER 6

Concierge Services

File under 'Great questions asked of Vacation Rental Staff'

Can we get tickets to whale watching boats on Moosehead Lake?

Bruce Porter, former owner
Northwoods Camp Rentals, Maine

Are there sharks in Lake Michigan?

Alan Hammond
Holiday Vacation Rentals, Michigan

Isn't it cute how all the boats park in the same direction?

Robert Frizzell
Boothbay Harbor, Maine

When deer grow up, do they become moose?

Bruce Porter, former owner,
Northwoods Camp Rentals, Maine

Do the islands go out with the tide, too?

Robert Frizzell
Boothbay Harbor, Maine

MARKETING: HAVING THE EDGE

A key factor in a vacation rental pro's success is their marketing ability. This involves finding the perfect blend of attracting clients (both homeowners and guests), utilizing advertising media, working with travel writers, and honing their presentation skills.

To find a successful vacation rental manager, the first step should be to ask around. Who do most people recommend? Do you see their signs frequently? Go to your local information center and check the printed material on the company. Look for them online and check their activity in social media.

PRESENTATION MATERIALS

Call several agencies and ask them to mail or email you their new owner information. If they don't have any, there's probably not a great marketing department in place – or maybe none at all.

From the information you receive, what appeals to you? Look for clear attractive graphics and simple explanations. Their materials should all have a certain "feel" about them and carry a consistent message.

Katie Wiberg of Vacation Cottages in Blue Hill, Maine says,

-    *"When comparing agencies, look for their advertising and the company's repeat business stats."*

If they market themselves well, they will be the ones that TV shows, travel writers and newspapers call on. Also ask professional people in other businesses and find out who they recommend and why.

If an agency markets itself well and does a good job operationally, they will have a high repeat business ratio. This is a very clear indicator of a company that is on the right track.

Where does the vacation rental professional you are considering advertise and what is their mix of print vs. web based or other media advertising. Their owner package should let you know this.

A good marketer will know the demographics on their clientele: where their guests come from, average age, economic levels, and most importantly what their guests are looking for.

Most companies will not put everything in their materials, but their presentation package and responses to your questions should leave you feeling you have made a good decision in going with them.

COMMUNITY INVOLVEMENT

Your chosen agency will have connections in the community with other businesses and be an active member of local business organizations. They will donate to local charities. Why? Well, not only is it a worthwhile thing to do, but effective marketing is often a byproduct of donating a weekend off season to regional PBS stations or other non-profit organizations for their events. Some of the events and charities Seaside has been a part of have included chamber events, PBS auctions, and local schools and sports teams. We have also initiated two "Heroes" programs we are very proud of.

The first occurred right after the devastation of the World Trade Center bombing. We contacted our homeowners who overwhelmingly offered time at their properties for the survivors' families and first responders. Within a year we started having those families arrive. And recently, we again asked our owners to step up to the plate and offer their places to veterans and their families. So far the programs have been a wonderful way for all of us, homeowners and staff, to give back.

James and Jacque Crouch are one of the recipients of our Heroes program. They were married and one week later, he was deployed to Afghanistan for eighteen months. We felt that time on the Maine coast was a wonderful way for veterans and their families to smoothly reenter their day to day lives with some great memories.

ADVERTISING

The advertising done for vacation rental properties needs to be simple, honest and consistent. If you are doing this yourself and not using a vacation rental professional, be very careful about unintentional use of terms that may be discriminatory.

Also be careful not to exaggerate the good points of the house or fail to mention the bad points. If it is not right on the ocean, for instance, do not advertise it as oceanfront – even if it has a great view. A good way to check an agency's marketing ability is to see how they are portraying homes in your area on their website.

If you decide to do vacation rentals on your own, you will need to decide on where the best place and time is to advertise. A choice I see often is print advertising in local papers during the high season. There are two flaws with that. First, guests who see your ad are already here and will not save the ad for the following year. Second, local papers do not reach your intended target in the area they live in. You need to determine the primary areas that vacationers travel from in order to advertise there. For example, if you have a house in the Blue Ridge Mountains, you'll probably want to advertise in Atlanta or if your house is on Cape Cod, you'll want to advertise in Boston, Hartford and New York.

Needless to say, web advertising and your own website are essential! If you are choosing to rent by yourself, you need to avail yourself of both. There are some really great do it yourself websites out there like Homeaway.com and VRBO.com. They do cost money, but it is money well spent if you are renting your property yourself.

However, if you are working with an agency, they probably go way beyond the do it yourself websites. An agency may additionally use a site like Homeaway, because of the exposure. Homeaway maintains a way of designating properties that are professionally managed. And although I mention Homeaway particularly, there are numerous sites out there.

PROMOTIONS

Another major part of marketing is using promotions. Travel writers or TV shows may expect a complimentary stay, but the coverage and future business received is well worth the loss of income for a short stay.

When your property is slow in renting, promotions are a useful tool in enticing someone to book. Maybe offering $50 gas cards when gas prices soar, or a gift basket, or restaurant gift certificate. Promotions can range from a free pen to offering discounts or specials to entice guests to book. At our company, each guest who checks in is given a tote bag with brochures of area information and coupons for many area businesses. Our guests love them, but they cost us very, very little. We have a big basket of small gifts for children and a table set up with refreshments.

For guests having a birthday or anniversary or other special event, it is a small cost but big benefit to deliver a small gift basket to them with a card.

This vacation rental manager may have a client for years to come because of it and so will you if you choose to rent your home with them.

One thing I don't recommend as a promotional item is key tags with the business name and address on the tag. Too often companies in their fervor to get their info out attach these tags to property keys with the property address or name. For safety reasons, this is just not a good idea. See the chapter on security for more information about this.

MAILINGS AND EMAIL BLASTS

Mailings and email blasts are another useful marketing tool. Agencies often target area businesses, former guests, and potential guests from leads lists. The longer an agency has been in business, the larger their leads list.

TAKE IT ON THE ROAD

Travel shows are offered all over the country and internationally. Thousands of people thinking of vacations go to these. A good vacation rental manager could be taking part in these and getting their info directly out to people attending, plus follow up with the leads generated by the show.

As an example, the Boston Globe Show has had 35,000 people attend. There are booths from all over the country and the world promoting their areas to visit.

If a tourism area and a good vacation rental company do their job, they will join forces and offer a giveaway of some sort – lobster dinner plus a weekend at a vacation rental property – and have attendees signing up for this. Those names are leads that can be contacted later.

A follow up with an incentive to vacation with your company may help them make the decision to rent with the agency.

Margaret Regan with daughter, Alexandra
At the Montreal Travel Show

New England VRMA booth at the Boston Globe Travel Show

PLAYING A NEW GAME

Working with other area businesses is just good common sense. If a guest comes to your area and finds plenty to do, good restaurants, services and cultural/historical venues that interest them, they will want to come back to vacation again. I've never understood those brochure racks in so many places that offer information on areas hundreds of miles from where that place is located. Why send your customer somewhere else?

Working with vendors who are involved with the vacation rental industry can add a lot of ideas to a management company as well. In the vacation rental industry these vendors include software systems, promotional materials, linens, hardware, locks, travel insurance, furnishings, amenities and much more.

Steve Zimmerman of Beach House Logos in Pittstown, New Jersey notes the huge increase in pet friendly properties from a decade ago when you had a really hard time finding one. His company which does many, many more promotional items has created a specialty. Steve says,

- *"We went out and hunted and searched for pet friendly products that we thought would be good for the industry and help companies brand themselves and market themselves. They saw their sales really take off as a result. If Maureen were going to rent the house, rather than having a package there that says the Regan family, there might be something that says "to Max Regan" who is a pet. The first thing they (the agency) do is ask the pet's name and then they put a little welcome package together for the pet. Information that has come back to us is that when they (the agency) treat this pet owner and the pet with such high regard they (the clients) have become an extremely loyal group to them. So our customers have helped us formulate the path we've gone on. While I might have had my idea of what I wanted to do there was a lot that got filled in between points A and point B that helped us get to where we are today. We developed a pet friendly program and there are probably about 40 or 50 agencies today that are buying pet friendly products that we deal with."*

Another person commenting on the value of the relationships between management companies and vendors in the industry is Ed Ulmer, Vice President of Barefoot Technology, in Henniker, New Hampshire. On that relationship's importance, he says,

- *"(The benefit of the relationship) depends on the market - like in the San Francisco market. Most of the folks that live in San Francisco are relatively high tech. If you want to be high tech, if you want to be leading the market you want to work with a vendor that is leading the market and is out there looking at other industries and seeing what they're doing and adapting from them to accommodate our little industry... and making it a little easier for you, the Vacation Rental Manager, you've got a very difficult job."*

PLAY FOR FUN

Marketing and customer service are often the same thing. Contacting guests to go over their needs when booking; smiling and offering ideas for good places to shop; writing a personalized note if an occasion arises; having the maintenance guy chat with the guest when he goes there to fix something – these customer service features are all elements of marketing as far as I'm concerned.

THE PRO'S MAKE THE BUCKS

THEY BOUGHT THE RIGHT EQUIPMENT

The simple fact is that in most cases, agencies have more money to invest in staff, marketing, customer service, training, software, advertising and the many tools and equipment that are needed to do vacation renting properly.

The agency may have invested in a commercial laundry facility. They have money to invest in additional items the guest may request. They may be able to offer a business center at their location; some companies offer facilities for corporate meetings, for events, even weddings and reunions.

Some agencies offer boat or kayak rentals or a multitude of other equipment relevant to the area. Just some of these items can include skis, snow mobiles and other winter vacation gear. The agency may have pre-purchased a large number of tickets to area attractions to obtain a discount for their guests.

MORE TO OFFER

A professional agency has probably invested in expensive, sophisticated software. They have a broad supply of maintenance tools.

Agencies with deeper pockets can better protect both guests and homeowners. The agency may have the tools and staff available to take care of things in the off season. They may have equipment that can traverse snow or handle storm situations including flooding issues. The fact that agencies have more money means that they may be able to solve problems more quickly.

Another benefit of having additional funds available is the ability to advertise and market better. Plus they can take advantage of last minute media promotions and offers.

CHAPTER 7

TECHNOLOGY IS THE NAME OF THE GAME

Need a Gas Mask?

A couple of years ago we had a skunk problem under one of our vacation homes. Our exterminator would not deal with the stinky critter, so we had our "low man on the totem pole" take up the task. Clay was working in our maintenance department and had been with us for about 6 months. He was 20 years old and we often described him as being like a Labrador puppy, full of energy and excitement, go, go, go. For him it was just another adventure. We had him dressed in a head to toe Tyvek body suit, an air mask (like the type used for painting), and safety goggles. His equipment was a have-a-heart trap filled with a turkey leg as bait. He crawled under the house with the trap and went back again a few days later and got the skunk and set him free far, far away. We should have taken a picture of Clay before he went out.

Betsy LaBarge, President
Mt Hood Vacation Rentals, Welches, OR

TECHNOLOGY
IS THE NAME OF THE GAME

A vacation rental professional is better equipped to handle rentals through the use of technology. And while homeowners have the basic items, the technology used in vacation renting today is much more industry specific than the basics. A successful manager will probably be using software designed to interface with a website, to allow people to view properties, check schedules, book online, generate reports, take care of the accounting, and see area information and much more.

WHAT A SWEET GAME

- *"Years ago when you talked, back then, about property management software you talked primarily about accounting and while that's certainly important, there are lots of other things that have emerged in recent years including websites and other related search technology that's involved with folks finding a property to rent, Facebook and the other social media, and those sorts of things."*

Peter Wenk, President, Virtual Resort Manager Software
Beaufort, North Carolina

The website should be well designed with software to allow bookings to happen in real time and to accept credit cards and much more. "Rent by owner" websites out there do offer these things. They do cost money. Most important to an individual doing their own rentals, these sites demand constant presence and oversight to be sure that every request is responded to quickly and calendars kept accurate.

Every step of the guest booking should follow a certain planned format. Send specific materials to the guest, then the guest is contacted with a standard follow up.

IT'S A RINGER!

Other types of technology that vacation rental pros use will include phone systems with extensions for different departments, a method of relaying information to a guest for emergency procedures, such as who to contact after hours (or the system might even automatically call a maintenance person). A vacation rental pro could use cell phones that allow departments to track time and work orders. An I-pad or notebook are technology that allow maintenance or cleaning departments to be able to punch in and punch out at each job, to record work order progress and let the reservations desk and others know when a property is ready for the guest.

Of course you, the homeowner, can use your phone in some of the same ways. The drawback to you, the homeowner, is that the phone number you are giving out is perhaps your personal cell phone or home phone! That is a number I would be hesitant, on a personal level, to give out to people I don't know. It feels a little too direct; it certainly compromises the homeowner's privacy and security.

SO MANY APPS, SO LITTLE TIME

Additional technology that can be used by vacation rental professionals are apps for cell phones to enable a potential guest to find the property on a map, find an agency's website and enable booking online through the guest's cell phone.

The mobile apps can also enable a homeowner to be able to enter the vacation rental company's website and find out what they have for bookings and how much money they have in their account; they can leave or read messages from the vacation rental pro.

Most vacation rental managers make active use of Facebook, Twitter and other social media and are able to quickly transmit what is available for rent, offering specials and promoting the company in general.

THIS GAME NEEDS REPAIR

Some of the other technology can be specialized tools for the maintenance department, or keyless entry locks to properties that allow a code or hotel type cards to be used for entry. There is so much technology, but it is an expensive option for a homeowner to invest in when they would doubtfully have enough properties to warrant that investment. Obviously I am only scratching the surface here of a huge variety of technology.

CHAPTER 8

ACCOUNTING FUNCTIONS: WHO'S KEEPING SCORE?

Follow the Money!

Eons ago when I first started in this business, credit cards were unheard of and all the guests paid cash when they arrived. Surprisingly, very few people cancelled at the last minute. But every Saturday after check in, my elderly Mom would drive her car behind my car as we took a large amount of cash to the bank's night depository. Her instructions were to toot her horn if anyone came into the lot while I was there. Unfortunately, her attention often wandered as I learned one night as I was putting the bank bag into the night drawer and someone tapped me on the shoulder and asked where they could go for a good lobster dinner!

Seaside Vacation Rentals, York, Maine

ACCOUNTING FUNCTIONS: WHO'S KEEPING SCORE

The next challenge to contemplate when making the decision whether to rent your place by yourself or to be part of a vacation rental management team is to look at the range of accounting requirements, Are you willing and able to do the numbers?

IT'S ALL ABOUT NUMBERS

To truly begin the rental process, you accept money from a guest, and then determine whether you'll accept cash or credit card, and decide how much needs to be deposited to make a reservation. Then when payments are made, where will that money will be kept. Is money received simply going to go in a family checking account or a separate account? If a separate account what restrictions are you going to put on checks to be written from it? This is a big decision for a homeowner to make and impacts the success of the rental venture from that point on. After you get paid for the rental, when does that money get disbursed to you? Is it after the rental has been completed that you take your money? Certainly there are a lot of questions to be answered.

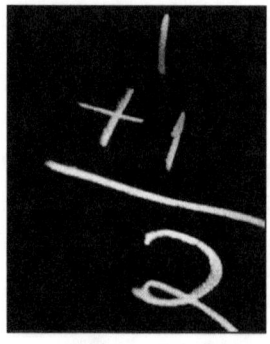

KEEP TRACK OF PAST NUMBERS

Record keeping should note income and disbursements and all the details. If you decide on an agency, your decision on a vacation rental manager should be made partly by learning the timeliness and detail of payments and statements that will be made to you. Each company prepares accounting somewhat differently and that is often dependent on the laws that govern the state they are operating in. Payments may be made with a portion in advance or they can be made in full after a reservation has ended. These are things that vary from place to place. However, the payments of these items and the timing of them should be made very clear up front to you. Then you can judge whether or not this can work for you.

NEW TWISTS

A vacation rental professional may be able to offer direct deposit of your payments and should offer statements on a frequent basis. They may also offer online access to statements and accounting information through their website depending on the software that they are using.

If you are renting the property yourself, another accounting function is the follow up for damages with security deposits. You will need to determine when and how much is to be returned to a guest. If there has been damage, what is the procedure in your state? Do security deposit returns have to be in writing with a breakdown of money for damages, and what kind of penalty is there, and how well was it been spelled out in advance on the lease for the person renting? With vacation renting, some agencies and homeowners who do it themselves hold a portion of security money to keep a reservation for the following year as a means of enticing the guest to return year after year.

This should be clear in their contracts and all parties should have some sort of acknowledgement of that.

WHAT'S MISSING

An often overlooked accounting function is to value your time as a factor in the rental process. As a homeowner, when considering the cost of using a vacation rental manager, you need to consider something that Cort Roussel from Franconia Notch Rental and Realty in Franconia, New Hampshire, said,

- *"The reality has to be measured against what the individual homeowner's personal hourly income is. You know, the value of the vacation rental manager really is determined more by the worth of the individual (homeowner) than by the manager themselves. In other words, for every hour that you as an individual homeowner put into answering an email, making a phone call, returning phone calls, those are hours added to your day because you already have your regular job. Or you've taken away from your day. And... wouldn't you rather be on a baseball field with your daughter or would you rather be answering email."*

Other accounting functions to be aware of:
   o Following up on unpaid rent payments
   o sending dunning letters to people who may not have paid in a timely fashion
   o setting definite timetables for payment
   o cancelling guest reservations if that timetable is not met or a good reason extended
   o the ability to accept credit cards
   o monitoring checks
   o Are the checks good or not, and if not what action needs to be taken.

One of the most important accounting functions is paying state, regional and local taxes that apply to vacation rentals. These need to be collected and monitored. Then that money must be reported and paid to the state, region or local government in a timely fashion.

If you are doing your own rentals, and you don't take care of taxes, you will be getting fined for non-reporting or under-reporting or even not doing it in a timely way.

The guest's perception of the competence and reliability of you or the agency is based on knowing where their money has gone and having verification. I think guests feel their money is safer with a company than with an individual they don't know.

The guest wants the ease and comfort of using any type of credit card when they make a reservation. This is frequently not something that homeowners who rent on their own can do.

GUARANTEED WINNER

Another accounting area that we haven't touched on is a vacation rental company's ability to offer travel insurance to guests, which may not be an option offered through an individual renting their own property.

These insurance policies allow guests to recover most or all of the money they have paid for a vacation if something happens like a bad storm, cancelled flights or if somebody becomes ill or dies and they can't come on vacation. Some of the travel insurances now even cover things like job loss. Life is uncertain and many unexpected things can go wrong, unfortunately. Travel insurance offers a great benefit to guests. Many rental companies also offer a damage waiver insurance or damage fee which covers what a security deposit has covered in the past.   These may cover the cost of damages incurred at the property accidentally with limitations.

SCOUTING FOR THE FUTURE

Accounting functions allow a good vacation rental manager or homeowner to stay on top of the business of vacation renting and may include spotting trends through accounting reports.   With vacation rental professionals, accounting reports allow them to see what has been happening in their business. They can answer questions such as: are people booking later, is the average price of a rental going up, down and more?

Reports allow a vacation rental company to do projections and budgets based on solid information. As a homeowner, you are using only one property and you can fall out of touch with what is happening in the industry as a whole in your area. You can miss out on some terrific opportunities this way. This can leave you isolated and without the edge.

The last accounting item to mention is end of the year accounting which you, the homeowner, receive from the vacation rental professional. Again this varies from state to state, but generally some sort of end of year accounting or a 1099 form is sent that allows you, the homeowner, to see what you have received for income across the year and expenses paid to the vacation rental company.
This makes it easier to file your income taxes. If you are doing your own vacation renting, you'll need to have all the records available for your tax filing. Thus accounting functions are crucial to maintaining profitability for you, the homeowner, as well as the vacation rental manager and providing security for the guest.

CHAPTER 9

SECURITY! WE'RE NOT PLAYING AROUND

The Bare Facts

A while ago, we received a call from an elderly couple who had brought their grandchildren on vacation. They wanted to know if we rented the three new oceanfront houses next to theirs that all looked alike. The reason she asked, was that her husband, who woke early had gone downstairs to make coffee and discovered a naked lady sleeping on the sofa. He went upstairs and woke his wife who came down and put a bath towel over the young woman. Grandma proceeded to wake the naked girl and ask who she was and what she was doing there. The young woman said absolutely nothing, but arose and dropped the bath towel and simply walked out the sliding doors onto the deck and lawn where the older couple saw her picking up piles of cloths she had dropped leading to their house. Their best guess and ours was that this young woman had confused the houses after some late night partying and just walked into the grandparents' house and crashed on the couch.

Of course, our handyman, Larry, commented "Wonder how long it took Grandpa to go upstairs and wake Grandma."

Seaside Vacation Rentals
York, Maine

SECURITY: WE'RE NOT PLAYING AROUND

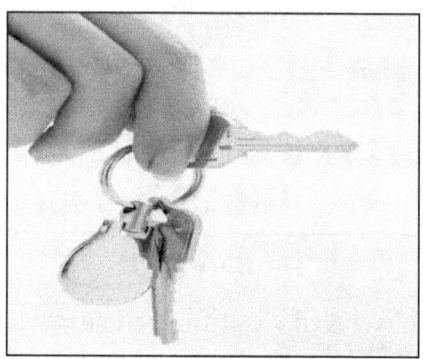

PROTECTING YOUR HOME

Security should be your most important consideration. You need to provide that security in many different areas. The first of those areas is the home itself. How do you keep your home safe and secure whether it is rented or vacant? You should have someone in that locale or a manager who can check on the property occasionally. This becomes really important during times when the home may be endangered by severe storms, winter conditions, flooding, other weather elements like brush fires, forest fires, and other conditions.

Besides having a person available to check, there are additional ways to monitor the condition of the property. You could invest in a security system as an option. Many of these systems contact you immediately if there is an intruder; let you know when the temperature drops to an unsafe level and more. But you still need to have someone go to the property and check it out.

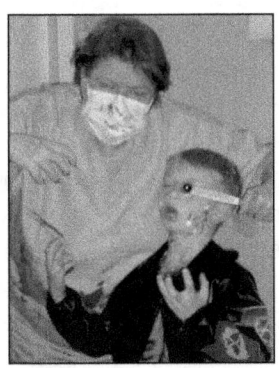

DON'T PLAY RECKLESSLY

Other areas of security concern the home's use as a vacation rental. If you are not using a professional, you need to decide how you will handle keys and access to your home for guests and for cleaners and others who may have to work on the property. It's extremely insecure to leave the key under a rock, or planter, or the welcome mat. Those would be the first places somebody trying to break into the property would check. Even in the safest of locations, issues can arise with vandalism or kids' entering a cottage that is unoccupied. There is a very real security risk to leaving a property unoccupied, unmonitored and having easy access to entry.

There is also a very real possibility of criminal activity. Somebody could break in and steal things. During these economically difficult times, thieves have gone as far as stripping out the copper piping and fixtures such as sinks and counter tops. Thus, security is definitely a high priority.

CAREFUL CONSIDERATION

Let's review security concerns for the guests. The handling of the keys is of paramount importance for the safety of people staying at your place.

As the homeowner, you could be considered liable if you are not handling the security of your rental property in a reasonable manner. Consider the scenario of a guest checking in who expected to find the property open or the key in a very obvious place, but somebody has broken in, or may still be there, or your guests arrive to a scene where the property has been destroyed. Not only would there be a question of owner liability, but the guest would suffer, whether they are injured personally or simply at risk of losing their vacation and peace of mind.

Having multiple keys in different locations or different people having keys creates an issue for the guest as well. I mean, can someone really sleep in peace knowing that everyone in town has a key to the property (maybe not knowing is even worse). So that's not a solution either.

PLAYING FOR MONEY

The security of the financial transactions is another factor that the vacation rental pro, the guest and the homeowner want to be assured is happening correctly. The money must be handled properly. If credit cards are used for the transactions and done online, there needs to be online security that will protect the guest from having his credit information stolen or used illegally.

Financial security also means that the homeowner must be assured they are going to get the money they earned from the rental of their home.

On the positive side, a vacation rental professional can provide security on all of these levels and more. They are usually located in close proximity to the property. Agencies have the ability to monitor the property, to be able provide services in cases of weather conditions, or to check on the property for the peace of mind of the homeowner and guest. Management should have secure transaction ability for the handling of money both online and in the office. They have staff or local contacts available that can provide what's necessary to maintain the security and integrity of the property.

For instance, let's say a storm comes along and breaks a sliding door into the house. The results are: the house gets soaked, is open to the elements, and perhaps the pipes freeze. By being able to check the property after a storm the vacation property manager would be able to provide glass service to repair the door so the house is secure. And the agency would report those things to you.

A VACATION RENTAL MANAGER PLAYS GOOD DEFENSE

Household security must apply to a guest in the same way. If they are staying in a property and a storm occurs, precautions should be in place. These may include notice of evacuation for major storms and hurricanes, or notifying the vacationer that windows must be taped and outside furniture put away or any number of other protective measures.

The guest may need to know about local shelters and when they can go back into the property and what to expect. This kind of service cannot always be provided by a homeowner and some agencies cannot do it either, but this is the ideal.

KEEPING THE PLAYERS IN LINE

An item for the homeowner's peace of mind is that the vacation property manager also has the ability to monitor the property's use and/or misuse and that includes some instances of when someone has broken the terms of their lease. With the agency's sign in front of the property, neighbors are usually more than willing to let the vacation rental manager know that there has been an infraction of the rules. Those rule infractions can include too many people, a party going on, loud noise, and too many cars. These issues, if they occur, are more easily handled by a vacation rental pro than the homeowner. A property manager may be able to avert having a small problem become a big one amongst your neighbors and the guests.

An amazing example of the monitoring of a storm goes to Alex Risser and his Social Media Coordinator at Outer Beaches Realty, in Avon, North Carolina. They went way above and beyond the call of duty and stayed on Hatteras Island during a hurricane. They were able to report and do video and pictures continually on what was happening during Hurricane Irene.

Their reports were even picked up on the national news. Obviously, there are great dangers involved with doing this, so this is not to be expected of every agency. But it is one of those cases of professionals going the extra mile.

- *"In the end, we had not only our Guests and Owners kept in constant communication with what was going on, but Owners and Guests of all the other companies as well. Many said we provided more in depth, accurate, and current reporting than any of the national or local news and weather sources. It has come back to roost as we have picked up significantly more new Property Management contracts going into next year as a result of recognition of what Outer Beaches Realty does during an event to keep it's customers informed every step along the way."*

Alex Risser, President
Outer Beaches Realty
Avon, NC

CHAPTER 10

ORGANIZATION MEMBERSHIPS

At a state meeting where a group of vacation rental agencies were grumbling about the difficulties they had encountered the previous summer, I asked a friend of mine, Bruce Porter, who used to own the Northwoods Camp Rentals business in Greenville, Maine, how he managed to keep his calm in this crazy business. Bruce looks like the epitome of the taciturn Mainer who lets absolutely nothing ruffle him. His reply was that he had been an air traffic controller for many years then a state trooper in Connecticut for many years, so he figured that if no one was shooting at him and no one was going to fall out of the sky, he could handle just about anything. I must say, I had to agree vacation rental problems seemed pretty tame after that!

Bruce Porter, Former owner
Northwoods Camp Rentals, Greenville, Maine

ORGANIZATION MEMBERSHIPS

OUT OF THE GATE

Memberships in regional and national organizations offer many benefits to companies in the vacation rental business. However, most national and regional vacation rental organizations, such as the Vacation Rentals Managers Association (VRMA), are open only to managers of properties they do not own personally. There are some other organizations that are open to individual homeowners renting their own property, also.

I think it is extremely important when a homeowner goes to choose a professional manager that the agency has an affiliation with a vacation rental organization. The primary reason this is important to you as a homeowner, is that you will reap the benefits of your vacation rental agency getting the best and most recent education and information on the market. The agency, by its membership, is also helping to promote the vacation rental industry as a whole, which in turn, helps you.

PASSING THE BATON

Membership in a vacation rental professionals group also allows the pro to be able to network, to be in touch with vendors. These groups are crucial to the learning aspect for professional managers. As well, they offer connections for the products that help a vacation rental run smoothly such as linens, promotional items, professional software to run their systems, keyless locks and a host of other items. As a homeowner, you may not have access to these vendors. If you do have access, you may not wish to order in the large quantities that these companies require.

If, for instance, you own one or two rental properties, you may find the correct vendor to buy six hundred thread count Egyptian linen from. Wow, the cost is lower than buying it retail, too. However, that vendor probably requires purchases by the case. This is not something that the average homeowner is going to do. It is simply not cost effective for someone who owns a couple of properties. But that may be one of the agency benefits of belonging to a national organization like the VRMA or another of its type.

Networking is another important aspect of organizational membership. But I would choose educational opportunities as the primary benefit of belonging to an industry specific organization.

'VRMA' stands for <u>Vacation Rental Managers Association</u>.

WHO ELSE CAN PLAY

What other organizations should your vacation rental professional belong to? They should be members of the local chamber of commerce or several area chambers if they are representing properties in more than one town. Better yet, they should not only belong to chambers, I think they should be active by volunteering, donating items to events, and serving in a leadership capacity for those chambers.

A homeowner considering an agency could check their membership in the Better Business Bureau. Some businesses choose not to belong to that group for cost reasons. But, any homeowner when weighing between one agency and another can check the Better Business Bureau to see if there have been complaints made against either agency and if the complaints were resolved. This provides a good indicator of the reputation of that company.

DON'T DROP THE BALL NOW

Beyond chambers, the Better Business Bureau and the VRMA, other organizations that a professional agency might belong to and that could be a benefit to the homeowner and the agency to become more professional are local and regional tourism boards and organizations. Tourism organizations are often formed when chambers or other groups get together on a regional, state or multi-state basis and share a direction. These tourism groups join together to do cooperative marketing and have a voice on governmental spending and other items.

This professional coalition has had increased importance to the vacation rental homeowner in the last 10-15 years because in some areas there has been increasing pressure to limit or curtail vacation rentals completely.

Organizations are able to speak to the financial impact of vacation rentals on a town. They often note the benefit of professionally managed vacation rentals in particular to address some of the concerns that local towns have about short term renting.

Town issues arising from vacation rentals are often based on properties that are not well monitored or are not managed by an agency but rather owned and rented by somebody who lives far away. And yes, these issues do occur with agencies as well.

Townspeople sometimes feel that an owner living in another location does not have a stake in their town, a reputation in the area, or the ability to monitor properties. Locals may feel that a business in the community has more reason to make sure that rentals run correctly. It comes down to reputation and a business being a part of a community. Preventing the curtailing of vacation renting means making sure the residents of that area understand the use of properties as vacation rentals and organizations, agencies and homeowners can all speak to that.

So, that's why membership by management companies in organizations including vacation rental groups, regional chambers, and tourism groups is important. Vacation rental homeowners then have a voice and the connections to turn to when local government seeks to inhibit or curtail vacation renting. Members of national organizations in other locations may have gone through the same problems and are able to offer advice to local vacation rental managers on how to speak out and what else to do in case of a movement to thwart vacation rentals.

WE CAN ALL WIN

I like what Leigh Clarke, Managing Director of Railey Mt Vacations in McHenry, Maryland, had to say about organization membership.

- *"What I would be looking for isn't membership but leadership."*

(You said it, Leigh!)

Another good reason for your local vacation rental manager to belong to organizations is that your agency connects with other businesses and is able to make them aware of the benefits of vacation rentals and how rentals impact each of their unique businesses.

For instance, we did a survey of our guests several years ago at Seaside. (We do one every year.) We learned that over and above the cost of rent, the average vacation group in a house which averages 6-8 people spent $3000.00-$5000.00 in the area throughout the week they rented. When we added it all up it accounted for $7 to $10 million going directly into the local economy.

Guests spent their money on restaurants, shops, attractions, gas, food, and many, many other local businesses.

Short Sands Beach, York, Maine

Believe me; other businesses do have a stake in the continuance of vacation rentals and in tourism. It trickles down to hardware stores or heating oil companies or the kids who do the lawns. They are all impacted by the vacation rental business.

Maybe the biggest factor used in addressing potential restrictions on vacation rentals is to point out the amount of money brought into a town government.

Homeowners with second homes, not just vacation rentals, in most tourist destinations pay the highest taxes because they are in closest proximity to major attractions such as ski slopes, lakes or the ocean.

The crazy part is that they often do not use their properties on a year round basis, so they don't impact the school system with additional children, and they don't utilize most of the town's services year round. In some cases, properties do not even have water and sewer in the winter, or trash pick up, or roads plowed. And these homeowners who may be paying 40% or more of towns' taxes don't even vote.

Vacation homes do not impact a town in a negative way financially, yet the community benefits in a very positive way from the amount of taxes that are collected from each vacation property, as well as benefiting from the vacation rental guests who are spending in the area.

Another interesting side note is that in Maine, a lot of the people who vacation in the area eventually buy here, retire in the area, live in the area later, and many of them start their own businesses and become an asset to the local communities.

CHAPTER 11

PROPERTY UPKEEP: FIT TO WIN

Clean out the Fridge!

"One of my funniest ones... You know when you get short handed, we all have done our share of cleaning houses and one day I had to go out and clean some houses and I thought I had done a good job and of course my staff is always willing to tell me I don't do as good a job as they do. They're always looking for an opportunity to point out where I might have messed up.

Well this one guy checked into one of the houses I had cleaned that afternoon. He called in and he said that there were some crumbs in one of the bins in the refrigerator and oh by the way did you know that the light in the refrigerator doesn't shut off when you close the door. I said there is no way that I would know that unless I climbed into the refrigerator and shut the door. How the heck does he know that? So my staff takes great pride in telling me this story."

Audrey Miller, Owner
The Cottage Connection, Boothbay, Maine

PROPERTY UPKEEP: FIT TO WIN

GAME ERRORS HAPPEN

While you might believe that you, as the homeowner, should be the sole entity in maintaining your property, this may not be entirely possible. Having a property used as a vacation rental offers specific challenges. You, the homeowner, have a very high standard of upkeep for your property and every vacation rental pro applauds that. However, renting for short terms in vacation areas entails a lot of use and quick turnover.

Guests are vacationing there to relax and have a good time, not to worry about the extra cleaning that an owner might do if the homeowner was there. Guests do not want to worry about misplacement of furniture, how they use things at the property, how much water they use, whether there is sand in their towel when they throw it in the washing machine, or a million other things. The guests are simply there to vacation. And even though the homeowner and the agency would love to be able to control some of guests' activities, it just isn't possible.

WE CAN BEAT 'EM

The good news is the vacation rental staff is usually there on a regular basis between rentals. Someone from the cleaning department goes into the property and does a cleaning to prepare the property for the next guest or the owner coming in.

The cleaning person and sometimes the departing guest will note if there is anything that needs the attention of the maintenance department like a dripping faucet, overflowing trash, plugged toilet, or light bulbs that need to be replaced.

Maintenance can then take care of whatever the problem is prior to the next person checking in.

There may also be an inspector who follows that cleaning person into the property to make sure that everything is as it should be, that the property is in move in condition, and there are no outstanding maintenance issues. In some cases, the same cleaning crew is assigned to the property every week, which means they can monitor if something is broken, missing, or damaged. The cleaning crew should be reporting to the office so the agency can follow up with the homeowner. Either the homeowner or the agency can then get an estimate of repair or replacement. The agency may send a check to the homeowner to take care of the item or the agency may get the replacement item so that the homeowner or the next guest is not inconvenienced when they arrive.

YOU CAN BEAT 'EM, TOO

Certainly any owner can do these things if they are in close enough proximity to make this feasible and desire to do so. Many homeowners hire a local cleaner to clean between rentals even if they use a vacation rental agency to manage. This is quite acceptable. However, there are occasionally issues with that solution from the vacation rental manager's perspective. Once guests have moved in, the guests might discover a flaw if the cleaning was not done properly. If the owner or their cleaner did the cleaning, then that person has to go out and redo the cleaning.

YET ANOTHER ERROR

Asking a cleaner to go back and redo a property is often not possible and universally never popular with cleaners, or for that matter, with homeowners, or anyone.

In the case of agency cleanings the housekeepers may be employees or subcontractors, but the agency has control over the cleaners. Because of that, sending an additional person out to take care of a problem is not a big deal like it is with an outside cleaning contractor or a homeowner.

It is difficult (to say the least) for an agency to call you, the homeowner, and inform you that the property was not cleaned well. If you live a great distance from the property, it certainly makes redoing the cleaning extremely difficult for you. When this happens, in most cases, an agency has to send some of their own people out and charge the owner for that, which is also never popular.

We have found over the years that there are many different acceptable levels of cleaning to different people. Simply asking the previous guest to leave it as clean as they found it just doesn't work. As an agency manager, I don't find this acceptable. Most vacation rental companies would have to say they are not perfect in the cleaning department, but I think the goal is to do more than just clean – the goal is to sanitize - particularly bathrooms and kitchens. An incoming guest should not have to worry about germs and/or dirt from a previous person.

Many people leaving a cottage who have been told to just leave it in the same condition will leave it in halfway decent condition but will certainly not scrub toilets and bathroom fixtures and so on.

That is something done by a cleaning crew. It is possibly the most important part of vacation rentals and each incoming guest has a right to expect true cleanliness. You wouldn't dream of staying in a hotel that had a policy of the last guest being responsible for cleaning, why would you consider it for your vacation home?

Cleaning is also a service that can be offered by the vacation rental professional to the homeowner when you use your property. Nothing puts a damper on staying at your own property more than having to scrub floors, bathrooms and kitchens the day you leave - and that goes for the homeowner as much as the guest. It's a great service that can be offered.

The training for cleaning staff is geared more towards hotel housekeeping than what you would expect from a friend using your cottage.

AND AN ISSUE, TOO

Another part of the upkeep on your property is the ability for an agency to inspect the property when it is not being used. This could be a simple walk through in the winter to check that pipes have not burst if there have been storms that have created a loss of power. It can also mean checking for critters prevalent in certain areas like raccoons or field mice. It is certainly a good idea to have somebody to lean on to inspect your property when you are not there.

Nubble Lighthouse, Cape Neddick, Maine

AND ANOTHER ROUND

Another important upkeep issue is that an agency has the ability to gather information from the rental guest that a homeowner may not feel comfortable in requesting.

If an agency has been in business for a number of years, a big chunk of their business may be from returning guests and referrals from those returning guests. Thus the agency has a built-in clientele that are usually quality vacationers and respect the properties they stay in. The agency wants feedback on the property and any needed upkeep so as to retain their guests.

Still another item on upkeep is that an agency is often able to do pool and hot tub maintenance, air conditioning and heating upkeep. They may be able to open and shut down the property's plumbing, offer spring cleaning, end of the season cleaning, and carpet shampooing. The agency may also have the ability to do renovations from minor things like painting a room to major renovations such as kitchen rebuilds, additions, adding a deck, hot tub, or other features that will make your property more desirable to rent and raise the rental price.

My belief is that overall; an agency is better equipped to handle the upkeep of your property, especially if you have a busy life – and who doesn't?

BEAT 'EM ALL

A great many homeowners choose to do the upkeep themselves which is fine as long as there is an understanding of the impact that this choice may have on you. Honestly, most agencies love a homeowner who does everything.

However, it may be worth its weight in gold for you to be able to be able to reach out to your vacation rental professional and say "I cannot be there to clean on August 20th because I have a wedding to attend. Can we schedule a cleaning for that particular date?" Or "I'm doing some work on the house this fall; can you get me a quote on tiling the bathroom?" Very often an agency will be able to accommodate you even if you usually do your own cleaning or maintenance.

CHAPTER 12

ETHICS & REPUTATION: KEEPING IT HONEST

Have a Heart

Our homeowners and staff have always responded to the opportunity to do a good deed. Everyone was impacted by the horror of the World Trade Center bombing on 9-11. One of our staff said, "Wouldn't it be a great thing if we could offer families of survivors and first responders a chance to spend time here on the Maine coast to help them heal." We all thought it was a wonderful idea and within minutes of emailing our owners, we had an overwhelming response from them offering their properties. That year we adopted a fire station in NYC and hosted families here. It was something that was accomplished by homeowners and our amazing staff acting as a team. We knew we had done something that mattered.

Seaside Vacation Rentals, York, Maine

ETHICS AND REPUTATION: KEEPING IT HONEST

BEING A GOOD SPORT

Most people are honest and ethical and value their reputation. However, in vacation renting the perception is that agencies are more likely to act in an ethical manner than individual owners due to pressure from other businesses, the law, their standing within the community, and with member organizations. This is not always true – there are dishonest, unethical agencies with bad reputations just as there are dishonest, unethical individuals. An agency's reputation, though, does make them more accountable and subject to reports on national websites and blogs where guests and homeowners can comment on the behavior of an agency. That can exert enough pressure to make an agency act in a more ethical way. An individual rental owner's misdeeds may go unrecognized or fall through the cracks, whereas an agency is more visible and may be held to a higher standard.

NO CHEATERS ALLOWED

Agencies who act in a dishonest and irresponsible manner are to be avoided at all costs. That is the main reason why homeowners and guests should check the reputation of the agency they are contemplating working with. Recently, in the news, there have been instances of agencies absconding with funds, leaving guests high and dry when they arrive for check in, homeowners who are not paid, or lied to about services performed, as well as agencies that have rented the property without permission and kept the money.

There are criminals in every walk of life and agencies are no more honest or ethical than anyone else. However, from the guest's perception an agency has more to lose than an individual homeowner.

An owner who doesn't do the right thing is going to lose one or more guests or face legal charges for not delivering what was promised. An agency can receive pressure from hundreds of guests and has a standing in the community that they don't want to lose or they shouldn't want to lose. They can also face fines and loss of licenses if they are real estate affiliated. This should make them more likely to follow higher standards when it comes to what they are doing. *It is absolutely necessary to check the agency you are contemplating working with whether you are a guest or homeowner.*

GAME OVERSIGHT IS KEY

So, from the perception of a guest, an agency is just a more reputable way to go. Especially these days when a guest could be renting without any safeguards to guarantee they receive what they have been promised. Nor do guests know if what they've been promised is even accurate. In some areas, vacation rentals have become a favorite target for scammers. Every agency, every homeowner and every guest should operate in the most highly ethical and honest fashion because it certainly comes back to you and word does get out that you are not someone to be trusted.

Whether you're a homeowner, guest or an agency, like your mama taught you, do the right thing and it will come back to you. This is a great rule to run your life by as well as a business.

Jennifer Thibodeau, Victoria Wyeth, Maureen Regan
Receiving a Family Business Honorable Mention award

Pat Eltman, Maine Tourism Director, Maureen Regan,
John Richardson, Maine Lieutenant Governor
Receiving Maine Governor's Award for Seaside's
contributions to Tourism

Margaret, Annette & Maureen Regan
Receiving Entrepreneur Award

Jennifer Thibodeau, Mike Clark, Robert Frizzell, Donna
Knoepfel, Maureen Regan
Receiving Best of the Best Award, fourth year in a row

Margaret, Annette & Maureen Regan
Receiving Maine Tourism Association Award

(Where else but Maine would you have a giant moose head
in the background?)

CHAPTER 13

VACATION RENTALS: REAL ESTATE OR A DIFFERENT GAME

Seaweed Removal Services

"Well we have many funny stories but the one which stands out the most is the lady who called one day all in a huff because there was 'seaweed' on her beach. When I picked up the phone all I heard was 'This is Jane from the ABC Cottage and I DEMAND to speak to the Seaweed Removal Service, NOW!' and I looked over at my fellow employee and smiled then said to the lady "Hold on, I'll put you through"

Katie Wiberg, President
Coastal Cottages, Blue Hill, Maine

VACATION RENTALS:
REAL ESTATE OR ANOTHER GAME

TUG OF WAR

This is an ongoing topic of conversation in the vacation rental community with advocates on both sides of the debate. Here are the basics.

There is no legal consistency in the way vacation rentals are handled from state to state. Vacation rentals in many states fall under the auspices and licensing of the real estate commission. In probably twenty five to thirty states, vacation rentals fall under general landlord/tenant law (sometimes in states with real estate licensing, sometimes in states without). In still other states, they fall under transient hotel law. So there is a real variety of how vacation rentals are treated from state to state.

- *"Why is it that when I stay somewhere 6 months and 1 day in the state of Florida I am under real estate guidelines and when I stay there 6 months I'm under the program (rental) laws. Why does that change what the property is? Is that a constitutional*

- issue that is on a macro scale versus a local government issue?"

Steve Trover, President of VRMA and
All Star Vacations in Kissimmee, Florida

Now you're probably asking yourself why this is important to a homeowner. There are many pros and cons to consider in this argument and you definitely need to know whether your state requires vacation rental agencies to be under the real estate commission or treats them in a different fashion.

Once we explore these issues further, it will become apparent that you, as the homeowner, have to know how those laws impact how homes are managed. And it does impact you and the guest ultimately.

REAL ESTATE TAKES ITS TURN

For states which fall under the control of the real estate commission for vacation rental professionals, the benefits may be that the vacation rental companies must be licensed, must adhere to a certain code of ethics, must adhere to real estate law, and are subject to fines if they do not comply with basic real estate rules and regulations.

Perhaps the greatest, most positive point in favor of this method of controlling vacation rentals is that a guest's money must be placed in a separate trust account. The "trust" account may be called a management account or holding account but basically it is a separate account set up from the operating funds that the vacation rental company uses to pay their bills and to pay themselves. The monies from that trust account are only allowed, by regulation, to be written to principals of the transaction.

For instance, a commission may be taken from that trust account and written to the agency and placed in the operating account, a check can be written from the trust account to the homeowner for the amount of money owed to them. If an agency collects security deposits, they go into the trust account and a check can only be written to the guest and/or the homeowner or the agency that did the work from the trust account depending on whether or not there were damages. These are the only principals that can receive a check from that account.

The trust account is bound legally and is a key element in protection of the homeowner and guest. This is one thing that most vacation rental agencies agree is a very positive side to operating under the real estate commission.

DRAWBACKS TO LETTING REAL ESTATE TAKE THE LEAD?

What are some of the negatives? Well, perhaps one of the biggest negatives is that vacation rentals are not really real estate. Factors that impact the sale of a property have almost no bearing whatsoever on the rental of a short term vacation property. When it comes to vacation rentals, most real estate commissions do not understand the nature of this strange creature that falls under their wing. That lack of knowledge impacts rules and restrictions on vacation rentals often negatively and can cause real estate commissions to be extremely restrictive concerning vacation rentals.

It also creates unnecessary barriers that vacation rental companies must overcome in order to operate efficiently. For instance, in the State of Maine, we do not fall under the real estate commission.

However if we did, when we advertised the real estate commission specifies the size of the font used in the name of the agency in relationship to anything else on an ad and how and what has to be placed on that ad. As well, there are a number of other things that go against real estate practices but are standard procedure for vacation rental advertising.

For example, sending out a mailing to certain homeowners to join your agency is not permissible. We would have to send a mailing to an entire area or town, not specific owners if they are working with another agency. If we had to follow real estate rules, it might not be possible to put the price of a vacation rental or mention that vacation rentals in general can go for example, a thousand dollars or under a week for a family of six. Maine real estate rules state that you cannot do that because you have to show a specific example of the price and break it down into all its details. These are just a couple examples.

So there are many hurdles built up that the real estate commission has created in the vacation rental industry. As you can probably tell, I am not a proponent of operating under the real estate commission.

The flip side is that following the economic downturn of 2008, many states in which vacation rentals did not fall under the real estate commission experienced agencies going out of business or floundering who used the "trust account money" - owner's money, the guest's money, to keep themselves afloat. They used it illegally and caused a great deal of pain to their homeowners, guests and others.

My feeling is that companies that are run by people who would do this would probably have had the same issues had their company fallen under the real estate commission.

However, it does seem that occurrences have been more prevalent in states where vacation rental management companies do not fall under the real estate commission. Many in the vacation rental industry feel there should be a separate oversight mechanism other than the real estate commission specifically for our industry.

IT'S IN-BOUNDS TO ASK ABOUT MONEY

How do you know whether or not the agency you are considering is one of these companies not treating their incoming money in a professional manner? I would simply ask if the agency has a separate trust account and how they handle their money, how the process works. That should be part of your interview with that vacation rental agency. It's kind of like going to a reputable doctor and asking questions about treatment and mentioning a second opinion to that doctor. Any professional physician would not have a problem answering questions and suggesting a second opinion. To a homeowner it should be a huge red flag if you run into an agency that will not answer your questions or if they find excuses why they do not operate in a manner to protect the money of a homeowner and guest.

If that agency has excuses as to why money is all dumped into one account that is a big red flag and you should seriously hesitate to use that company.

Another plus for being under the real estate commission is that there are more legal controls over the agency. But the negative is that many of those controls are not relevant to vacation rentals. Unfortunately, the reality is that many traditional landlord/tenant legal options and real estate rules are totally irrelevant to this industry. As I have stated before, there is a huge gap of knowledge by most real estate commissions about the vacation rental industry.

For instance, even if an agency falls under the real estate commission, they may be subject to eviction laws that are focused on long term traditional landlord/tenant law which just does not fit this kind of rental. Just think about the eviction process in a long term rental; the entire eviction process can take anywhere from six months to a year. If somebody should refuse to leave a vacation rental property at the end of a week the necessity of using that kind of option is insane. It is devastating not only to the home-owner but to every other guest who may be scheduled to come into that property as well as the agency.

But perhaps the solution in the states where vacation rentals come under the real estate commission is to make those commissions more knowledgeable about vacation renting and change the makeup of the commissions to include more members that do vacation renting.

THIS IS A DIFFERENT GAME ENTIRELY

This industry is a cross between the hotel industry and traditional home renting and may have a little bit of real estate thrown in. It really is a different animal than most states determine it to be. When an agency is in a state that falls under the real estate commission or under traditional long term renting laws, that state is really not designed to work with vacation rentals.

Alan Hammond, President of Holiday Vacation Rentals, in Harbor Springs, Michigan says,

- *"While I am an advocate of good regulation, I don't believe that real estate licensing would be the best approach for the vacation rental industry regulation in Michigan. Vacation rentals are a hospitality business where rental managers have guests, not customers or clients. Real estate is a transactional business whereas vacation rentals are a service business with a transaction component. The value of the transaction is much different when purchasing a home than when renting a few days or weeks.*

- *The industry more closely aligns with hotels and resorts providing accommodations and experiences for guest enjoyment during their leisure time.*

- *I believe that a new licensing category other than real estate would better serve the industry and protect the consumer. Because rental managers have an agency agreement with a property owner to provide services and collect and handle rent belonging to the owner, I believe that trust accounting requirements used under real estate licensing should become a regulated practice of vacation rental managers."*

Some states that have huge numbers of vacation rentals have been successful in making some of their unique issues heard. North Carolina operates under the real estate commission, but has specific rules governing vacation rentals. Florida does not operate under the real estate commission, but vacation rental companies there have successfully had some laws changed to cover the vacation renting industry.

A serious option for the future of this industry is to have a national organization that is strong enough to set rules and regulations and to police their membership like realtors.

They could be a force for lobbying the interests of the vacation rental business as well. Many leaders within the industry advocate for this approach.

WHO MAKES THE RULES

Many industry people I've interviewed feel that the nature of the primary organization, the Vacation Rental Managers Association and the role they play will in time, change dramatically.

They feel it will have more control and influence on the industry. Once there is more universal certification of vacation rental managers, homeowners will be able to know if an agency manager is educated and equipped to handle the business.

Interviewees also feel that the Vacation Rental Managers Association may move towards being a voice to lobby for more cohesive structure across not only the country but internationally. With one primary voice to lobby either for or against laws that may impact this industry, the organization can help to design the way the industry is perceived and build in safeguards protecting guests, homeowners and the vacation rental professional.

CHAPTER 14

GOING IT ALONE: PLAYING SOLITAIRE

Royal Flush

I received a call at 11:30pm one night from guests who were experiencing a septic system back up – really not a pleasant thing. They had one bathroom and 2 little children. However, they were not my guests! The owners of the property had, unknown to me until that time, rented the property themselves. When I called to tell them of the problem, they were very upset and practically begged me to help them out. They didn't have to beg, I just kept thinking of that poor family with no bathroom and sewage backing up into the house. I called my best buddy, the septic system guy, and he picked me up at my house around midnight and I took him down several nameless dirt roads to the cottage. I waited and consoled the family while the septic tank was pumped, then cleaned the bathroom for them with loads of bleach. When we finished, it was about 2:00am. The homeowners, Tony and Helen, never again rented on their own.

Seaside Vacation Rentals
York, Maine

GOING IT ALONE: PLAYING SOLITAIRE

So, let's summarize.

When you choose a vacation home, what is your goal for it? Are you planning on using it yourself much of the time and only want to fill in weeks by renting? Are you looking at it as an investment and want to rent everything and make it as profitable as possible? Do you want to resell it in a few years? Are you looking at renting for five or ten years then you will move into it when you reach retirement age? Your first decision is to determine what your goals are as this will greatly influence your choice of a property.

ARE YOU SURE YOU WANT TO PLAY THIS GAME

The whole experience of renting it yourself is potentially fraught with many obstacles and dangers. From the very beginning choosing the correct property in the right location is difficult. Then you need to match your goals to the preferred rental property with a certain number of bedrooms and baths. Do you choose a home or condo? Is the area you are considering mostly family oriented? If so, perhaps a 3-4 bedroom house with multiple baths and a first floor bedroom and bath for an elderly person is the ideal. If the area you are considering is an upscale area that primarily attracts young professionals, then perhaps one bedroom or two bedroom places are your best bet. Perhaps you choose a high rise condo on the beach or go for a large older luxury home overlooking the water. These questions are usually answered when you use a vacation rental manager.

WHERE TO START

Your choices as you start out are very important.

If your real estate professional doesn't understand vacation rentals, they may not be looking at the same criteria that a vacation rental specialist would be. They are looking only for real estate value.

I'll give you an example from the area I live in. We have a very beautiful historic part of town, but not on the water, I'll call the "village". There are lovely older homes with large land holdings and they are absolutely spectacular, however, they do not rent as vacation rentals. For our vacation guests they are just too far from the beach. That also goes for other really nice areas which have no beach.

Area realtors would say that your best real estate value is buying something in either the "village" or the other areas. However, from a vacation rental standpoint, they are your worst choices because they will not rent or will only rent at giveaway prices and with great difficulty. A seasonal cottage without a basement that is less than a block to the beach will win out over a lovely year round home a few miles from the beach if vacation rental income is your goal.

Without a vacation rental professional, you may not be getting the right house if vacation rentals are your goal.

Your real estate agent should be working with a vacation rental professional to assist you in fulfilling your goals.

WHY DON'T YOU HAVE A COACH ON YOUR TEAM

If you bought a place without assistance from a vacation rental professional and are fortunate enough to get the right size, location, and proper amenities, the next step is deciding on rental price.

This may be somewhat easier than it used to be with all the websites that help individual homeowners to do their own vacation renting. However, there is still some difficulty.

You can see what price places are advertised for, but you do not see what they actually rented for. It's kind of like checking comparable properties when a house is for sale. The homeowner says, "Gee, the guys down the street have their house listed on the market for $500,000." The key factor that a realtor or vacation rental manager knows is that they have it listed for sale, but have not yet sold it. $500,000 may be just wishful thinking on their part.

The main item in determining sale price is what has "sold". That is why you need to know what prices vacation rental properties actually get booked for in your neighborhood and in the same type of property as yours. Your vacation rental professional is going to be your best resource for this.

The reason this is so important is that if you are renting your house yourself and you overprice your home, you may book several weeks and then have many weeks of vacancies. Having a situation where you get brief periods of rentals and then multiple weeks' vacancy will obviously harm your bottom line. These issues pretty much go away when you use a vacation rental manager.

NOT HAVING ALL THE CARDS

On the other hand, under pricing your rental place will allow you to fill all your weeks, but you are leaving money on the table that could be in your pocket. Plus you'll find it very difficult to raise your prices the next year if people

want to re-rent your house. And who wouldn't want to re-rent if the place is priced under the market value?
It's hard to say no to people who have already rented it.

The next thing to do is to market your property. There are websites out there that can assist you with this if you are renting the property yourself. You can also advertise it at work or you may have family members who want to rent it. They'll say, "Oh, we go to the beach there on vacation every year and we'd love to rent it". Let me share with you how difficult this situation can be.

First of all, if you rent your property yourself, and are dealing with family or friends, it is very hard to place yourself in the position of demanding a certain amount of money up front. Plus you need to get a security deposit. Can you then enforce payment from them? And, at the very end, if something has gone wrong, you will have to hold their security deposit money. This can lead to the end of a friendship, a strained work relationship, or extremely tense Thanksgiving dinners with your family. It's a really tough situation to be in. However, it can be done and many times it works out just fine. These issues pretty much go away when you use a vacation rental manager.

I DIDN'T WIN, BUT NO ONE KNOWS

If you are renting your own property, from a financial standpoint, you need to be very firm and businesslike and this can be hard for some people, especially when you hear a hard luck story. You may be moved to make exceptions to your own rules. It is wonderful to have a buffer like a vacation rental pro between you and your guest. It means that you won't be taken advantage of by well meaning people who don't view your situation as a business. We know you want to be hospitable to your family, friends and co-workers; however, your situation is that you need to rent this to pay your mortgage, taxes or other expenses until you retire or fulfill other plans for the house.

You really should not make deals that decrease the price you normally get in any substantial way unless necessary. Very difficult to do when dealing with people you know. Imagine if your sister/brother offers you $500.00 per week instead of that $1000.00 you are asking. How do you say no? If you do say no, then the negotiations start, "how about if I give you $100.00 now and $50.00 per week?" Then they miss a payment and you are stuck playing the bad guy which can damage your relationship.

These examples give you a feel for what obstacles there are so that you will be well aware of what you could be up against should you decide to go it alone and rent your own vacation rental property. These issues pretty much go away when you use a vacation rental manager.

I WON, I WON, BUT NO ONE KNOWS

You are renting your own property. Let's say you are all booked up and you are happy with the price you're getting. The next thing is how you will handle the transfer of keys, the check in and checkout process? You could plan on meeting the guest at the house at a certain time. That is one way to do it. However, they may not arrive until quite late at night, so you'll have to have a way to accommodate them without threatening the security of the guest or the house by leaving the house unlocked and keys on the table.

The other issue is that people are supposed to check out at a certain time and may be slow to leave.

You would then be left without enough time to clean and prepare the property for the next person checking in. And heaven forbid the next person checks in early!

But let's say all goes well with the check in and checkout process. So, how the keys are handled is yet another consideration in check-ins and check outs. This issue goes away when you use a vacation rental manager.

I WON, BUT I DIDN'T WIN

You are renting your own property. What are your plans if something goes wrong while there are guests in the house? These things can range from mild inconvenience to serious life threatening situations. Minor things could be that the place wasn't cleaned to the guest's satisfaction. If you do the cleaning, you'll have to re-clean the house. Or you disagree with the guest and say that the property was fine when I left, you must have made the mess. (I guarantee that this approach won't be appreciated☺).

Other minor inconveniences could include the coffee carafe has a crack and can't be used or the toaster isn't working, there are no utensils for the grill. If you don't live nearby these requests can be a huge problem. If you do live nearby, it can be extremely annoying and frustrating to have people knocking on your door or calling you every day with different minor requests. These annoyances, for the most part, go away when you use a vacation rental professional.

And if we go back to consideration of your perfect property, you need to know upfront how to equip that house.

It takes a vacation rental professional to know what kinds of things guests will be looking for and they can often give you an inventory list of what to stock in your new vacation rental home. These issues pretty much go away when you use a vacation rental professional.

NOTHING WORKS IN THIS GAME

Some of the major catastrophes that have happened in my 30 year career in this business have ranged from gas leaks to power outages to no heat in the winter, to hurricanes, toilets that don't work, septic systems that back up in the middle of the night. There is no question that you can handle these things, but the point is do you want to?

I cannot stress enough the importance of having a manager in the local area. In the case of most vacation rental professionals they have a list of resources that they have used that they can call such as plumbers, electricians and the rotor-rooter man. For years, the rotor-rooter man and I have been on a first name basis.

These skilled professionals get a great deal of work from the vacation rental company, but they will most likely get only the one job from you. That doesn't mean that they won't be happy to get the work from you, but you are an unknown and in the back of their mind, they wonder if they will have to wait or have problems collecting their money. In some cases, some professionals demand payment in advance, so you may still have to travel to where your property is.

Your accounting will need to include taxes. First, find out if your state charges lodging/sales tax on rentals (and many states do). You must collect these taxes over and above the cost of the rental amount and submit it monthly to your state and/or town tax offices.

This is a very key and important part of the vacation rental work. It is always easier for a professional business to do this than an individual. Bear in mind that if you don't do this, you are breaking the law and subject to enormous fines. It is certainly not something to play around with.

Second, your income taxes at the end of the year need to accurately reflect your expenses and income on the property. And of course, your guests want accurate and up to date accounting of what they have paid and what they may owe. These issues pretty much go away when you use a vacation rental professional.

GEARING UP FOR NEXT SEASON

Now you are at the end of your vacation rental season. You've got wear and tear on your property. Glasses are missing, marks on the wall, the washer needs repair. You will need to separate yourself from this and remind yourself that you are in a business venture where you need to put a percentage of everything you make back into the property. In any type of renting, you will need to replace items and upgrade on a frequent basis to continue to get top dollar. I usually suggest homeowners put 10% of their income back into their home. These issues can be helped tremendously when you use a vacation rental manager.

Now you have the score, How do <u>you</u> want to play the rental game?

RESOURCE GUIDE
BY STATE

Alabama Coastal Properties, Inc.
Orange Beach, AL
seeyouatthebeach.com

Aronov Condo Management
Gulf Shores, AL
Martinique-Gulf.com

Gulf Shores Vacation Rentals
Gulf Shores, AL
gsvacationrentals.com

Kaiser Realty, Inc.
Gulf Shores, AL
kaiserrealty.com

Mandoki Hospitality
Gulf Shores, AL
Mandokihospitality.com

Sanders Beach Rentals
Hartford, AL
sandersbeachrentals.com

Sunset Properties
Gulf Shores, AL
sunsetproperties.com

Young's Suncoast Vaca Rntls
Gulf Shores, AL
youngssuncoast.com

Hot Springs Vacation Rentals
Hot Springs, AR
arkansascondos.com

Pegasus Solutions
Scottsdale, AZ
http://pegs.com

Westbrook Vacation Rentals
Phoenix, AZ
wdpvacationrentals.com

ChaletsatBigWhite.com
Kelowna, BC, Canada
chaletsatbigwhite.com

Snowebb Services, Inc.
DBA Rentchalets
Kelowna, BC, Canada
rentchalets.com

AE Hospitality
Los Angeles, CA
aehospitality.com

Agate Bay Realty, Inc.
Carnelian Bay, CA
agatebay.com

AGreatPlaceToStay.net
Capitola, CA
aGreatPlaceToStay.net

Barbara McLain Props
Carlsbad, CA
barbaramclain.com

Beach House Rentals
Capitola, CA
beach-houserentals.com

Beach Rentals
Gualala, CA
searanchrentals.com

Beachfront Only Vaca Rntls
Oceanside, CA
beachfrontonly.com

Better Vacation Rentals
Cardiff by the Sea, CA
bettervacationrentals.com

Burr White Realty
Newport Beach, CA

Catalina Island Vaca Rntls
Avalon, CA
catalinavacations.com

Cayucos Vacation Rentals
Cayucos, CA
cayucosvacationrentals.com

CENTURY 21 Ditton RE
Oakhurst, CA
basslakevacations.com

Coast Getaways
Mendocino, CA
coastgetaways.com

Coastal Properties
Santa Barbara, CA
coastalrealty.com

Coasting Home, Inc.
Gualala, CA
CoastingHome.com

CSA Travel Protection
Campbell, CA
csatravelprotection.com

Dave Stubbs Real Estate, Inc.
Solana Beach, CA
VacationBeachHomes.com

Gold Rush Resort Rentals
Northridge, CA
goldrushresortrentals.com

HD Supply Facilities Maint.
San Diego, CA
http://hdsupplysolutions.com

HereStay, LLC
Danville, CA
herestay.com

Home 2 San Francisco
San Francisco, CA
home2sf.com

Idyllwild Vacation Rentals
Idyllwild, CA
idyllvacationrentals.com

Jenner Vacation Rentals
Jenner, CA
jennervacationrentals.com

La Jolla Vacation Rentals Ca
La Jolla, CA
lajollavacationrentalsca.com

La Quinta Vacation Homes
La Quinta, CA
LQVacations.com

Lake Tahoe Accommodations
South Lake Tahoe, CA
tahoeaccommodations.com

LeisureLink
Pasadena, CA
leisurelink.com

Monterey Bay Property Mgt
Monterey, CA
montereyrentals.com

Mountain Hospitality Svcs
Mammoth Lakes, CA
mammothfrontdesk.com

MyVR
San Francisco, CA
myvr.com

MyVRMS
Shingle Springs, CA
myvrms.com

PayByGroup
Mountain View, CA
paybygroup.com

Payment Processing, Inc.
Newark, CA
paypros.com

Perfect Places
Los Altos, CA
perfectplaces.com

Pinnacle Lake Tahoe Getaways
South Lake Tahoe, CA
laketahoegetaways.com

Plumas Pines Vacation Homes &
Rentals
Blairsden, CA
plumaspinesrealty.com

RE/MAX Yosemite Gold
Groveland, CA
yosemitegoldvacations.com

Rental Guardian LLC
Irvine, CA
RentalGuardian.com

Russian River Vacation Homes
Guerneville, CA
riverhomes.com

San Carlos Agency, Inc.
Carmel, CA
sancarlosagency.com

Sanctuary Vacation Rentals
Pacific Grove, CA
sanctuaryvacationrentals.com

Sandiegovacation.com
Imperial Beach, CA
sandiegovacation.com

Sandy Vacations LLC
Chino, CA
sandyvacations.com

Shaver Lake Vacation Rntls
Shaver Lake, CA
shaverlake.com

Shoreline Vacation Rentals
Fort Bragg, CA
shorelinevacations.com

Snowcreek Resort
Mammoth Lakes, CA
snowcreekresort.com

Sonoma Vacation Rentals
Healdsburg, CA
sonomacountyvacations.com

Southern California Vaca. Rtls
La Jolla, CA
socalvacationrentals.com

Tahoe Keys Resort
South Lake Tahoe, CA
tahoevacationguide.com

Tahoe Moon Properties
Tahoe City, CA
tahoemoonproperties.com

Tahoe Mountain Resorts Ldg
Truckee, CA
tahoemountain lodging.com

Vacation Palm Springs RE
Palm Springs, CA
vacationpalmsprings.com

Vacation Rentals of the Desert
Palm Desert, CA
vacationrentalsofthedesert.com

VacationRentPayment
Walnut Creek, CA
vacationrentpayment.com

Valerie's Vacation Rentals
Tustin, CA

Allegiant Management
Winter Park, CO
.alpineresortproperties.com

Alpine Edge Property Mgt
Breckenridge, CO
alpineedgebreck.com

Ascent Processing, Inc.
Boulder, CO
ascentprocessing.com

Black Canyon Inn, Inc.
Estes Park, CO
blackcanyoninn.com

Blizzard Internet Marketing
Glenwood Springs, CO
blizzardinternet.com

Blue Tent Marketing
Carbondale, CO
bluetent.com

East West Resorts - Beaver Crk
Avon, CO
eastwestresorts.com

Evolve Vacation Rental Network
Denver, CO
http://evolvevacationrental.com

Exclusive Vail Rentals Vail CO
Golden, CO
exclusivevailrentals.com

Frias Properties of Aspen
Aspen, CO
friasproperties.com

Guest Research, Inc.
Greenwood Village, CO
.guestresearch.com

GuestStream, Inc.
Denver, CO
gueststream.com

HDR Homes
Denver, CO
hdrhomes.com

HotSpot Tax Service
Greenwood Village, CO
hotspottax.com

Key to the Rockies
Keystone, CO
keytotherockies.com

Leddy Associates, Inc.
Aspen, CO

LockState
Denver, CO
lockstate.com

Macnaught, LLC
Carbondale, CO
macnaughtllc.com

McCartney Property Mgt
Aspen, CO
mccartneyproperties.com
MDM Group Associates
Steamboat, CO
mdmgroup.net

Range Property Mgt
Estes Park, CO
rangeprop.com

Resort Data Processing
Vail, CO
resortdata.com

Resort Managers
Breckenridge, CO
breckenridgeresortmanagers.com

ResortQuest Breckenridge &
Keystone
Breckenridge, CO
resortquestbreckenridge.com

ResortQuest Telluride
Telluride, CO
resortquesttelluride

Ski Colorado Vacation Rntl
Fort Collins, CO
skicoloradovacationrentals.com

SkyRun Partners, LLC
Golden, CO
skyrun.com

Vail Resort Rentals, Inc.
Vail, CO
vailresortrentals.com

Vacation House Review
Washington, DC
vacationhousereview.com

Jack Lingo, REALTOR
Rehoboth Beach, DE
jacklingo.com

Long & Foster R E OC Sq.
Bethany Beach, DE
LFVacations.com

ResortQuest Delaware
Bethany Beach, DE
resortquestdelaware.com

Wilgus Associates
Bethany Beach, DE
wilgusassociates.com

360 Blue, LLC
Santa Rosa Beach, FL
360blueproperties.com

All Star Vacation Homes
Kissimmee, FL
allstarvacationhomes.com

Amenity Services, Inc.
Destin, FL
amenityservicesinc.net

Anna Maria Gulf Coast Rntl
Holmes Beach, FL
amgcrentals.com

At Home in Key West Inc.
Key West, FL
athomekeywest.com

Award Vacation Homes
Clermont, FL
awardpoolhomes.com

AYP Rentals
Sunny Isles Beach, FL
ayprentals.com

Beach Reunion
Destin, FL
beachreunion.com

Beach Time Rentals
Clearwater, FL
beachtimerentals.com

Beachview Vacation Rentals
Destin, FL
beachviewvacationrentals.com

Cabin Fever Vacations
Fort Myers, FL
cabinfevervacations.com

Carter Beach Property
Miramar Beach, FL
destin-vacation-rental.com

Cocoa Beach Best Inc.
Cocoa Beach, FL
cocoabeachbest.com

Collins Vacation Rentals
St. George Island, FL
CollinsVacationRentals.com

Emanagement, LLC
Kissimmee, FL
nowrentme.com

Endless Summer Realty
St. Augustine, FL
endlesssummerrealty.com

Excellent Vacation Homes
Kissimmee, FL
excellentvacationhomes.com

Florida Dream Homes
Kissimmee, FL
FloridaDreamHomes.com

Florida Vacation Beach Rntl
Vero Beach, FL

Glad to Have You, Inc.
Santa Rosa Beach, FL
gladtohaveyou.com

Global Resort Homes
Kissimmee, FL
globalresorthomes.com

greatoceancondos.com
Winter Park, FL
greatoceancondos.com

Holiday Isle Properties
Destin, FL
holidayisle.net

IQware, Inc.
Deerfield Beach, FL
iqwareinc.com

Jan Doughty CPA PLLC
Cocoa Beach, FL
JanDoughtyCPA.com

JMC Resort Properties, LLC
Clearwater Beach, FL
JMCResortServices.com

Kennedy Training Center
Hollywood, FL
Kennedytrainingcenter.com

Keys Holiday Rentals
Islamorada, FL
KeysHolidayRentals.com

Kingfisher Vacations, Inc.
Sanibel, FL
vacationkingfisher.com

Lahaina Island Accms
Ft. Myers Beach, FL
beachtime.us

Luxury LifeStyle Vacation Hms
Davenport, FL
LuxuryLifeStyleVacationHomes.com

Magical Memories Villas
Kissimmee, FL
magicalmemories.com

MHB Property Management
Cape Coral, FL
capecoral4vacation.com

Miami Habitat
Miami Beach, FL
miamihabitat.com

Naples Florida Vacation Hms
Naples, FL
NaplesFloridaVacationHomes.com

Navarre Properties, Inc.
Navarre Beach, FL
navarrelistings.com

Newman-Dailey Res. Props
Destin, FL
DestinVacation.com

Ocean Properties & Mgt
New Smyrna Beach, FL
OceanProps.com

Ocean Reef Club
Key Largo, FL
oceanreef.com

Paradise Properties
Sarasota, FL
paradisevacationproperties.net

Premier Sotheby's Intl RE
Naples, FL
rentnaples.com

Realtech Services, Inc.
Lakewood Ranch, FL
rtservices.net

Reef Rentals
Key Largo, FL
reefrentals.com

Rent Key West Vacations
Key West, FL
rentkeywest.com

Rent Sunny Florida
Clermont, FL
rentsunnyflorida.com

Rental Network Software
Bradenton, FL
rental-network.com

Resort Rentals Inc.
St. Pete Beach, FL
resortrentals.us

Resort Vacation Prop's of
St. George Island
St. George Island, FL
rvpsgi.com

ResortQuest NW FL
Ft. Walton Beach, FL
resortquestNWFL.com

Royal Shell Vacations
Sanibel, FL
RoyalShell.com

Scenic Properties Luxury
Vacation Homes
Santa Rosa Beach, FL
scenicpropertiesfl.com

Scurto Marketing
Destin, FL
scurto.com

Sea Star Property Mgt
Fort Myers, FL
seastarvacationrentals.com

Starmark Vacation Homes
Celebration, FL
starmarkvacationhomes.com

Sterling Resorts, LLC
Destin, FL
Sterlingresorts.com

Sun Palace Vacations
Fort Myers Beach, FL
sunpalacevacationhomes.com

Sunset Reflections Vaca. Rntls
Cape San Blas, FL
sunsetreflections.com

Vacation Rntl Pros Prop Mgt
Ponte Vedra, FL
vacationrentalpros.com

Villa4uflorida
Kissimmee, FL
villa4uflorida.com

VillaDirect Management
Kissimmee, FL
villadirect.com

VIP Vacation Rentals LLC
Sanibel Island, FL
vip-vacationrentals.com

Water Street Hotel
Apalachicola, FL
waterstreetholtel.com

Waterfront.com, LLC
Miami Beach, FL
waterfront.com

American Associated Co's
Fayetteville, GA
directlinensource.com

Cabin Rnt of Helen & Sautee
Helen, GA
renthelen.com

Cabins For You, LLC
Taylorsville, GA
cabinsforyou.com

Escape to Blue Ridge
Alpharetta, GA
EscapetoBlueRidge.com

Georgia Mountain Rentals
Sautee, GA
georgiamtnrentals.com

Hodnett Cooper Vaca. Rntls.
St. Simons Island, GA
hodnettcooper.com

Mattress Safe, Inc.
Cumming, GA
mattresssafe.com

Mermaid Cottages
Tybee Island, GA
mermaidcottages.com

Oceanfront Cottage Rntls
Tybee Island, GA
oceanfrontcottage.com

Sandy's by the Shore
Tybee Island, GA
sandysbytheshore.com

ScenicRentals.com
Roswell, GA
ScenicRentals.com

Tybee Joy Vacation Rentals
Tybee Island, GA
tybeeluxuryrentals.com

Tybee Vacation Rentals
Tybee Island, GA
tybeevacationrentals.com

Vacation Rental Photography
St Simons Island, GA
vacationrentalphotography.com

Captain Cook Resorts
Honolulu, HI
CaptainCookResorts.com

Destination Resorts Hawaii
Wailea, HI
drhmaui.com

Great Vacation Retreats
Koloa, HI
greatvacationretreats.com

Hawaii Beach Homes Inc.
Honolulu, HI
sandsea.com

Kohala Coast Properties
Kailua-Kona, HI
kohalacoastpropertiesinc.com

Murdock Vacation Rentals
Kapolei, HI
murdockvacationrentals.com

The Parrish Collection Kauai
Koloa, HI
parrishkauai.com

Tropical Villa Vacations
Kihei, HI
tropicalvillavacations.com

Cayman Condos
Nashua, IA
cicondos.com

DoneRight Management
McCall, ID
donerightmanagement.com

High Country Resort Rentals
Sun Valley, ID
highcountry-rentals.com

LiveRez Inc.
Boise, ID
liverez.com

Valet Vacation Rentals
Donnelly, ID
valetvacationrentals.com

DVD-NOW
Burr Ridge, IL
dvdnowfreemovies.com

HomesRetreat.com
Chicago, IL
homesretreat.com

Protect-A-Bed
Wheeling, IL
protectabed.com

Vacation Storebuilder
Skokie, IL
VacationStorebuilder.com

AMJ Insurance
Indianapolis, IN
associationmembersinsurance.com/vrma

Bose McKinney & Evans
Indianapolis, IN
boselaw.com

Global Connections, Inc.
Overland Park, KS

Atlantic Vacation Homes
Gloucester, MA
atlanticvacationhomes.com

CapeCodRentals.com
Orleans, MA
capecodrentals.com

Flipkey, Inc.
Boston, MA
flipkey.com

John C. Ricotta & Assoc.
Chatham, MA
chathamrentals.com

Leighton Realty Rentals
Brewster, MA
LeightonRealtyRentals.com

New England Vacation Rentals
Harwich Port, MA
newenglandvacationrentals.com

Coldwell Banker Deep Creek RE
McHenry, MD
deepcreekrealty.com

Eastern Shore Vacation Rentals
Easton, MD
easternshorevacations.com

Long and Foster Real Estate, Inc.
Deep Creek
McHenry, MD
deepcreekresort.com

Mouse On House, Inc.
Berlin, MD
mouseonhouse.com

OffLake Rentals
Oakland, MD
offlakerentals.com

Railey Mt. Lake Vaca.
McHenry, MD
deepcreek.com

Shoreline Properties Inc.
Ocean City, MD
shorepro.com

Taylor-Made Deep Creek Vaca
McHenry, MD
deepcreekvacations.com

Vacation Rental Video
Garrett Park, MD

Vantage Resort Realty
Ocean City, MD

Visual Data Systems
Columbia, MD
vdsys.com

Camden Accommodations
Rockport, ME
camdenac.com

Coastal Cottages
Blue Hill, ME
vacationcottages.com

Cottage Connection of ME
Boothbay, ME
cottageconnection.com

MaineStay Vacations
Orr's Island, ME
MaineStayVacations.com/

Morton & Furbish Vaca Rntls
Rangeley, ME
rangeleyrentals.com

Northwoods Camp Rentals
Greenville, ME
mooseheadrentals.com

Seaside Vacation Rentals
York, ME
seasiderentals.com

Your Island Connection, LLC
Bailey Island, ME
mainerentals.com

Blue Fish Vacation Rentals
Union Pier, MI
bluefishvacations.com

Holiday Vacation Rentals
Harbor Springs, MI
holidayvacationrental.com

Lakeshore Lodging, Inc.
Saugatuck, MI
lakeshorelodging.com

Mill Pond Realty, Inc.
Saugatuck, MI
millpondrealty.com

Shores Vacation Rentals
South Haven, MI
shoresvacationrentals.com

Visit Up North Vacation Rntls
Traverse City, MI
VisitUpNorth.com

Whirlpool Corporation
Benton Harbor, MI

Cascade Vacation Rentals
Tofte, MN
cascadevationrentals.com

InCircleRentals, LLC
St Louis Park, MN
InCircleRentals.com

ResortsandLodges.com
Cottage Grove, MN
resortsandlodges.com

Crystal Water Villas
Gravois Mills, MO
crystalwatervillas.com

StoneBridge Resort
Branson West, MO
stonebridgebranson.com

Leadify
Jackson, MS
leadify.net

Big Sky Luxury Rentals
Big Sky, MT
bigskyluxuryrentals.com

Five Star Rentals of Montana
Whitefish, MT
fivestarrentals.com

Mountain Home –
Montana Vacation Rentals
Bozeman, MT
mountain-home.com

Yellowstone Property Mgt
W. Yellowstone, MT
yellowstonepropertymanagement.com

Alan Holden Realty
Holden Beach, NC
holden-beach.com

Atlantic Beach Realty Inc.
Atlantic Beach, NC
atlanticbeachrealty.net

Atlantic Realty
Kitty Hawk, NC
AtlanticRealty-nc.com

Bald Head Island Ltd Prop.Mgt
Southport, NC
baldheadisland.com

Beach Realty - Kitty Hawk Rntls
Kill Devil Hills, NC
beachrealtync.com

Bluewater Associates
Emerald Isle, NC
bluewaternc.com

Brindley Beach Vacations
Corolla, NC
brindleybeach.com

Brunswick Plantation
Golf Resort
Calabash, NC
brunswickvillas.com

Bryant Real Estate
Wrightsville Beach, NC
bryantre.com

Bryson & Associates, Inc.
Surf City, NC
brysontopsail.com

Carolina Beach Realty
Carolina Beach, NC
carolinabeachrealty.net

Carolina Designs Realty
Duck, NC
carolinadesigns.com

Carolina Mornings, Inc.
Asheville, NC
carolinamornings.com

Carolina Shores Vaca. Rntls
Kill Devil Hills, NC
outerbankscarolinavacations.com

Cashiers Resort Rentals
Cashiers, NC
cashiersresortrentals.com

Century 21 Action, Inc.
Surf City, NC
century21topsail.com

Century 21 Coastland Realty
Emerald Isle, NC
coastland.com

Coldwell Banker Spectrum Prop.
Atlantic Beach, NC
spectrumproperties.com

Cooke, REALTORS
Ocean Isle Beach, NC
cookerealty.com

Corolla Classic Vacations
Corolla, NC
corollaclassicvacations.com

Emerald Isle Realty, Inc.
Emerald Isle, NC
EmeraldIsleRealty.com

Great Smokys Cabin Rntls
Bryson City, NC
4GSCR.com

Greybeard Realty
Montreat, NC
greybeardrealty.com

Hatteras Realty, Inc.
Avon, NC
hatterasrealty.com

Hutchins Allen & Co.
Kitty Hawk, NC
obxcpa.com

Identify Yourself
Kitty Hawk, NC
identifyyourself.biz

Intracoastal Realty
Wrightsville Beach, NC
intracoastalrentals.com

Island RE by Cathy Medlin
Surf City, NC
topsailvacation.com

Jenkins Rentals
Blowing Rock, NC
jenkinsrentals.com

Local Social, Inc.
Holded Beach, NC
localsocial.biz

Margaret Rudd & Assoc.
REALTORS
Oak Island, NC
rudd.com

Moneysworth Beach Home
Equipment Rental
Kitty Hawk, NC
mworth.com

Mountain Country Cabin Rntls
Murphy, NC
mountaincountrycabinrentals.com

Mountain Lake Rentals
Glenville, NC
mountain-lake-rentals.com

Ocracoke Island Realty
Ocracoke, NC
ocracokeislandrealty.com

Outer Beaches Realty
Avon, NC
outerbeaches.com

Pirate's Cove Vacation Rentals &
Property Mgmt.
Manteo, NC
pirates-cove.com

Red Sky Travel Insurance
Kitty Hawk, NC
redskyinsurance.com

RentABeach
Surf City, NC
rentabeach.com

Rental Sentry
Holden Beach, NC

Resort Realty of the Outer Banks
Nags Head, NC
resortrealty.com

ResortQuest Outer Banks
Corolla, NC
resortquestouterbanks.com

Seaside Vacations
Kitty Hawk, NC
seasiderealty.com

Sloane Realty Vacations
Ocean Isle Beach, NC
sloanerealty.com

Solupay Payment Sol.
Wake Forest, NC
solupay.com

Southern Shores Realty Co
Kitty Hawk, NC
southernshores.com

Stan White Realty & Const.
Nags Head, NC
outerbanksrentals.com

Sun Realty of Nags Head
Kill Devil Hills, NC
sunrealtync.com

Sunset Properties, Inc.
Sunset Beach, NC
sunsetproperties.travel

Sun-Surf Realty
Emerald Isle, NC
sun-surf.com

The Vacation Bridge
Beaufort, NC
thevacationbridge.com

Topsail Realty, Inc.
Topsail Beach, NC
topsail-realty.com

Twiddy & Company,
Duck, NC
twiddy.com

United Beach Vacations
Carolina Beach, NC
unitedbeachvacations.com

Village Realty Rentals
Nags Head, NC
villagerealtyobx.com

Virtual Resort Manager
Beaufort, NC
VirtualResortManager.com

Ward Realty Corporation
Surf City, NC
wardrealty.com

Wendy Wilmot Properties
Bald Head Island, NC
wendywilmotproperties.com

Williamson Realty, Inc.
Ocean Isle Beach, NC
williamsonrealty.com

Wright Property Mgt
Kitty Hawk, NC
wpmobx.com

Barefoot Tech.
Henniker, NH
barefoot.com

Bayside Rentals
Meredith, NH
baysiderentalsnh.com

Franconia Notch Vaca.
 Rental & Realty
Franconia, NH
franconiares.com

Loon Reservation Svc
Lincoln, NH
loonres.com

Mittersill Alpine Resort
Franconia, NH
mittersillresort.com

Preferred Vacation Rntls
Moultonborough, NH
Preferredrentals.com/vrm

Victorex, Inc.
Henniker, NH
victorex.com

Beach House Logos
Pittstown, NJ
beachhouselogos.com

Eric Mason Consulting
Hackettstown, NJ

HomeStead Real Estate
West Cape May, NJ
homesteadrealestate.net

Ocean Beach Rental
Lavallette, NJ
oceanbeachnj.com

RealTimeRental.com
Ocean City, NJ
realtimerental.com

Silicon Travel
Bayonne, NJ
silicontravel.com

The TomK Consulting Grp
Jersey City, NJ
TomKConsulting.com

Wyndham Exchange and Rntls
Parsippany, NJ
wyndhamvacationresorts.com

Kokopelli Property Mgt
Santa Fe, NM
kokoproperty.com

Lantern, Thredbo
Thredbo, NSW, Australia
lanternapartments.com.au

Incline at Tahoe Realty
Incline Village, NV
InclineAtTahoe.com

Sun Cabo Vacations
Carson City, NV
suncabo.com

Bravo Holiday Residences
New York, NY
bravovillas.com

Coldwell Banker Whitbeck
Associates
Lake Placid, NY
coldwellbankerwhitbeck.com

Finger Lakes Premier Prop.
Penn Yan, NY
fingerlakespremierproperties.com

Howard Hanna Holt RE
Mayville, NY
howardhannaholt.com

Roomorama.com
New York, NY
roomorama.com

Island Club Rentals
Middleburg Heights, OH
islandclub.com

The Energy Butler
Northfield, OH
theenergybutler.com

All-Season Cottage Rentals
Halliburton, ON, Canada
haliburtoncottages.com

Cottagelink Rental Mgt
Havelock, ON, Canada
clrm.ca

Demeure
Waterloo, ON, Canada
demeure.com

Holiday Rentals
Toronto, ON, Canada
holidayrentals.ca

Interactive Vacation Rental
Owen Sound, ON, Canada
rentcottage.com

All Seasons Property Mgt
Welches, OR
mthoodrent.com

Bella Beach Property Mgt
Depoe Bay, OR
bellabeach.com

Bennington Properties
Sunriver, OR
benningtonproperties.com

Black Butte Ranch
Black Butte Ranch, OR
BlackButteRanch.com

Cannon Beach Vaca Rntls
Cannon Beach, OR
visitcb.com

Discover Sunriver Vaca. Rntls
Sunriver, OR
discoversunriver.com

Meredith Lodging
DBA Beachfront Rentals
Lincoln City, OR
beachfrontrentals.net

Mt Hood Vacation Rentals
Welches, OR
mthoodrentals.com

NAVIS
Bend, OR
TheNavisWay.com

Oregon Beach Vacations
Portland, OR
oregonbeachvacations.com

PointCentral
Bend, OR
pointcentral.com

Sand and Sea
Seaside, OR
sandandseaoregon.com

Seaside Vacation Homes
Seaside, OR
seasidevacationhomes.com

Sisters Vacation Rentals
Sisters, OR
sistersvacation.com

Sunray Vacation Rentals
Sunriver, OR
sunrayinc.com

Vacasa
Portland, OR
vacasarentals.com

Grosfillex, Inc.
Robesonia, PA
grosfillexfurniture.com

Kaba Ilco inc
Montreal, QC, Canada
kabakeylesslocks.com

Luxury Retreats Mgt
Montreal, QC, Canada
luxuryretreats.com

Atwood Vacations
Edisto Island, SC
atwoodagency.com

Beach Props. of Hilton Head
Hilton Head Island, SC
beach-property.com

Beachside Getaway
Hilton Head Island, SC
beachsidegetaway.com

Beachside Vacations
Isle of Palms, SC
beachsidevacations.com

Beachwalker Rentals, Inc.
Johns Island, SC
beachwalker.com

Booe Realty
Myrtle Beach, SC
booerealty.com

Commendable Rentals
Georgetown, SC
commendablerentals.com

DeBordieu Rentals
Georgetown, SC
DeBordieuRentals.com

Dunes Realty
Garden City Beach, SC
dunes.com

East Islands Rentals
Isle of Palms, SC
eastislandsrentals.com

Elliott Luxury Rentals
North Myrtle Beach, SC
elliottluxuryrentals.com

Etcetera, Inc.
Myrtle Beach, SC
etcmb.com

Fripp Island Resort
Fripp Island, SC
frippislandresort.com

Garden City Realty
Garden City Beach, SC
gardencityrealty.com

Harbor Linen
Rock Hill, SC
harborlinen.com

Hilton Head Accom.
Hilton Head, SC
hiltonheadusa.com

Hilton Head Rent Direct
Hilton Head, SC
hiltonheadrentdirect.com

Hilton Head Rntls & Golf
Hilton Head, SC
hiltonheadvacation.com

Hilton Head Vacation Rntls
Hilton Head Island, SC
800beachme.com

Interactivity Marketing
Myrtle Beach, SC
InteractivityMarketing.com

Island Realty
Isle of Palms, SC
islandrealty.com

Litchfield Real Estate
Pawley's Island, SC
litchfieldrealestate.com

Palmetto Dunes Oceanfront
Hilton Head, SC
palmettodunes.com

Palmetto Sands
Hilton Head Island, SC
palmettosands.com

Pawleys Island Realty Co
Pawleys Island, SC
pawleysislandrealty.com

Performance Development
Corporation
Hilton Head Island, SC
performancedevcorp.com

Pertnear, Inc.
Hilton Head, SC
pertnear.com

Resort Rntls of Hilton Head Isl.
Hilton Head Island, SC
hhivacations.com

ResortQuest Charleston
Kiawah Island, SC
resortquest.com/vacation-rentals/south-
carolina/charleston

Resortquest Hilton Head Isl.
Hilton Head Island, SC
resortquesthiltonhead.com

ResortQuest Myrtle Beach
Myrtle Beach, SC
resortquestmyrtlebeach.com

Savannah Getaways
Pickens, SC
savannahgetaways.com

Seaside Vacations
(North Myrtle Beach)
North Myrtle Beach, SC
seasidevacations.com

Sunset Rentals Inc.
Hilton Head, SC
sunsetrentals.com

The Lachicotte Company
Pawleys Island, SC
lachicotte.com

The Vacation Company
Hilton Head Island, SC
vacationcompany.com

Thoms Real Estate, Inc.
/Century 21 Thomas
North Myrtle Beach, SC
century21thomas.com

Vacation Rentals of
 North Myrtle Beach
North Myrtle Beach, SC
vacationrentalsofnmb.com

Venture Resorts, Inc.
Columbia, SC
ventureresorts.com

Black Hills Vacation Homes
Lead, SD
blackhillsvacationhomes.com

Exec. Ldg. of the Black Hills
Deadwood, SD
Executive-Lodging.com

Accommodations by
 Sunset Cottage
Pigeon Forge, TN
sunsetcottage.com

American Patriot Getaways
Pigeon Forge, TN
patriotgetaways.com

Aunt Bugs Cabin Rentals
Pigeon Forge, TN
auntbugs.com

Auntie Belham's Realty &
Nightly Rentals
Pigeon Forge, TN
auntiebelhams.com

C2G Advisors, LLC
Franklin, TN
c2gadvisors.com

Cabins USA LLC
Pigeon Forge, TN
cabinsusa.com

Chalet Village Properties
Gatlinburg, TN
chaletvillage.com

Dollywood Vacations
Pigeon Forge, TN
dollywoodvacations.com

Fireside Chalets LLC
Pigeon Forge, TN
FiresideChalets.com

Internet Marketing Exp. Grp
Sevierville, TN
imegonline.com

Jackson Mountain Homes
Gatlinburg, TN
JacksonMountain.com

Mountain Laurel Chalets
Gatlinburg, TN
MtnLaurelChalets.com

Mountain Rntls of Gatlinburg
Gatlinburg, TN
mountainchalets.com

Norris Lake Cabin Rentals
New Tazewell, TN
norrislakecabinrentals.com

Oak Haven Resort, Inc.
Sevierville, TN
OakHavenResort.com

RiverStone Resort &Spa
Pigeon Forge, TN
riverstoneresort.com

Snowman Rentals
Franklin, TN
snowmanrentals.com

Timber Tops, LLC
Sevierville, TN
yourcabin.com

BRIC Vacation Rentals
Laredo, TX
bricrental.com

Choice Hospitality Sol.
Frisco, TX
choicehospitalitysolutions.com

Cinnamon Shore Rentals
Port Aransas, TX
cinnamonshore.com

Cobb Real Estate, Inc.
Crystal Beach, TX
cobbrealestate.com

DepositGuard
Austin, TX
depositguard.com

HomeAway for Property Mgrs
Austin, TX
homeaway.com

HomeAway Software for
Professionals
Austin, TX
software.homeaway.com/vacation-rentals

Lake Travis Vacation Rentals
Spicewood, TX
laketravisvacationrentals.com

Miss Kitty's Fishing Getaways
Rockport, TX
rockporthomerentals.com

Padre Island Rentals
South Padre Island, TX
pirentals

Prudential Gary Greene
Galveston, TX
prudentialgalveston.com

Rainman
Boerne, TX
rainman.com

Ritenergy International
Plano, TX
ritelock.com

Ryson Vacation Rentals
Galveston, TX
sellinggalveston.com

Sand 'N Sea Properties
Galveston, TX
sandnsea.com

Starkey Property Mgt
Port Aransas, TX
starkeyproperties.com

VacationList.com
Little Elm, TX
vacationlist.com

Brian Head Vaca Rntls
Brian Head, UT
vacationbrianhead.com

Future Focus Utilities
Salt Lake City, UT

Park City Lodging, Inc.
Park City, UT
parkcitylodging.com

Snow Flower Property Mgt
Park City, UT
snowflowerparkcity.com

Utah Vacation Homes
Salt Lake City, UT
utahvacationhomes.com

Vacation Quest, Inc.
Park City, UT
vacation-quest.com

VacationRoost
Salt Lake City, UT
vacationroost.com

Allstar Lodging
Luray, VA
allstarlodging.com

Atkinson Realty
Virginia Beach, VA
atkinsonrealty.com

Bay Creek Resort Rentals
Cape Charles, VA
baycreekresortrentals.com

Chincoteague Resort Realty
Chincoteague Island, VA
chincoteagueresort.com

Dockside Realty
Lake Anna, VA
docksiderealty.com

Sanctuary Realty at Sandbridge
Virginia Beach, VA
sanctuaryresortva.com

Sandbridge Realty, Inc.
Virginia Beach, VA
sandbridge.com

Siebert Realty
Virginia Beach, VA
siebert-realty.com

Catered To Vacation Homes
St John, VI
cateredto.com

Cimmaron Property Mgt
St. John, VI
cimmaronstjohn.com

GetAway Vacations, Inc.
Killington, VT
getaway-vacations.com

Killington Group (TKG Inc)
Killington, VT
killingtongroup.com

Mount Snow
West Dover, VT
mountsnow.com

Slopeside Okemo Condo Rntls
Ludlow, VT
slopesideokemo.com

Stowe Country Homes
Stowe, VT
stowecountryhomes.com

Wise Vacation Rentals
Killington, VT
wisevacations.com

CDA Vacation
Spokane, WA
cdavacation.com

CondoBids, Inc.
Bothell, WA
condobids.com

Seabrook Cottage Rentals
Pacific Beach, WA
seabrookwa.com

Vacation Internationale
Bellevue, WA
viresorts.com

Vacations by the Sea
Westport, WA
vacationbythesea.com

Veranda Beach Resorts
Oroville, WA
verandabeach.com

Keefe Resort Rentals
Lake Geneva, WI
keeferealestate.com

Rent One Online
Stevens Point, WI
rentoneonline.com

Sand County Service Co
Lake Delton, WI
sandcounty.com

The Conger Collection, Inc.
Waunakee, WI
thecongercollection.com

Travel Guard Travel Ins
Stevens Point, WI
travelguard.com/vacationrentals

First Tracts
Snowshoe, WV
firsttracts.com

Jackson Hole Resort Ldg.
Teton Village, WY
JHresortlodging.com

Akumal Properties
Akumal North, Mexico
akumal-villas.com

Amsterdam City Apartments
Amsterdam, Netherlands
amsteramcityapartments.com

Aruba Villa Rentals
/Caribbean Sun Villas
Bakval, Aruba
ArubaVillaRentals.com

Bizflats
Barcelona, Spain
bizflats.com

Casamundo GmbH
Hamburg, Germany
casamundo.de

CBT Ltd
Beckenham, United Kingdom
razorpms.com

Gold Coast Villas Aruba
Malmok, Aruba
arubacondorentals.org

Lifestyle Villas
S. De R.L. de C.V.
Cabo San Lucas, Mexico
lifestylevillas.net

Luxury Villa Collections
Cabo San Lucas, Mexico
luxuryvillacollections.com

McLaughlin Anderson Lux Vill
St. Thomas, Virgin Islands
mclaughlinanderson.com

Mead Brown Costa Rica
Puntarenas, Costa Rica
meadbrown.com

Paradizo
Barcelona, Spain
paradizo.com

Paris Be A Part of It
Paris, France
paris-be-a-part-of-it.com

Rental Butler
Jolly Harbour, Antigua & Barbuda
rentalbutler.com

RenteGo
Prague, Czech Republic
rentego.com

ResortQuest Whistler
Whistler, ON, Canada
resortquestwhistler.com

The Hoseasons Group
Earby, United Kingdom

VIVA Villas Inc.
St John, Virgin Islands
vivacations.com

Organizations

Better Business Bureau
bbb.org

OTTI
Office Travel & Tourism
otti@trade.gov

Runaway Getaway Alliance
runawaygetaway.com

US Chamber of Commerce
uschamber.com

HomeAway
HomeAway.com

U.S. Department of Comrc.
Int'l Trade Admin/OTTI
1401 Constitution Ave, NW #1003
Washington, DC 20230
202-482-0140
tinet.ita.doc.gov

**VRMA, Vacation Rental
Managers Association
9100 Purdue Road, Suite 200
Indianapolis, IN 46268
Ph: 317-454-8315
vrma.com**

We were unable to include
all the companies and
organizations in this guide.
**Those who contributed to
the book are bold.**

Cape Neddick, Maine

HOMEOWNER'S SCORECARD FOR
THE RENTAL GAME
Winning with a Professional Vacation Rental Team

Please respond to each question with a score of 1 to 10. "10" means you or the agency can definitely do this the best. You can split your answer if you have abilities in certain areas, for example, you might put a score of "6" for your own ability to market, and agency "A" might score a "4". Always be sure the total is "10" for each question, however.

Now add up each score. How do you want to play The Rental Game? Do you do it yourself? Or do you think you could be Winning with a Professional Vacation Rental Team?

	QUESTION	DO IT MYSELF	PRO AGENCY "A"	PRO AGENCY "B"
1	Do I honestly have the time to take on renting my property myself?			
2	Do I have the education, training and skills to rent my property myself?			
3	Can I handle the hospitality and customer service aspects of vacation renting by myself?			
4	Am I able to do the best job of marketing and advertising my property myself?			
5	Will I invest in the technology needed to rent my property myself?			

	QUESTION	DO IT MYSELF	PRO AGENCY "A"	PRO AGENCY "B"
6	Am I willing and able to tackle the accounting functions necessary to do vacation rentals myself?			
7	Am I able to see to the security of my property and my guests and the transactions of vacation renting?			
8	Will I be able to reap the benefits of organizational memberships for my vacation rental?			
9	Am I able to manage the upkeep of my property in all ways by myself?			
10	Overall, do I want to do this, or be part of a team approach with a professional vacation rental management company?			
	TOTALS			

For more information on professional vacation renting or to order copies of this book, visit **www.the-rental-game.com.**

www.ingramcontent.com/pod-product-compliance
Lightning Source LLC
Chambersburg PA
CBHW051522170526
45165CB00002B/575